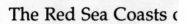
The Red Sea Coasts o

The Red Sea Coasts of Egypt

Sinai and the Mainland

Jenny Jobbins

Color Photographs by Thomas Hartwell

The American University in Cairo Press

Publisher's Note
Every effort has been made to ensure that this book is accurate at the time of going to press, but we hope that users will help us update and improve it for future editions by notifying us of any changes or relevant new information. Please write to or call: The Editor, The American University in Cairo Press, 113 Sharia Kasr el Aini, Cairo. Tel: 357-6892.

Dar el Kutub No.4307/89
ISBN 977 424 206 8

Printed in Egypt by International Press

Contents

Illustrations

Maps and Plans

Acknowledgments

I should like to thank the officers of the Ministry of Tourism, especially Selma Arida in el-Tor and Baghdady Hamed in Hurghada; Zeyad el-Bassell and Frances Carter of Cairo Divers; Chris McKinley for his comments on the geology of the Red Sea, and Mahmoud Kenawi for his help in Hurghada; also Mary Megalli, Marianne Mitchell, Jan and Ahmed Sherif, and Ihab Badran for their company and driving skills; Tom Hartwell for making final revisions to the text; and finally the many kind friends in Cairo and up and down the coast who contributed information, advice, and practical help.

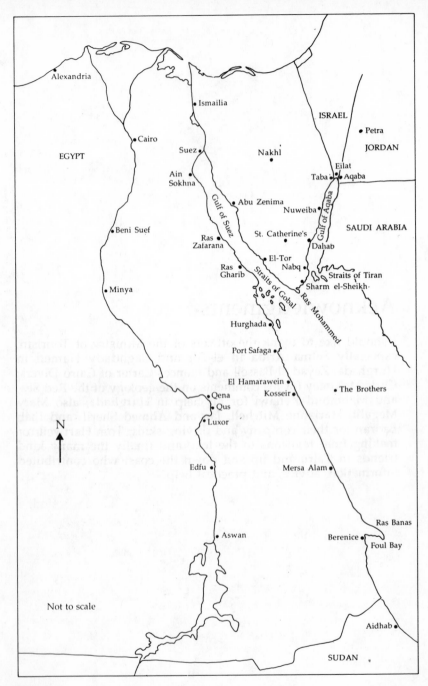

Egypt

Introduction

Tucked away at the top of the Red Sea lies a string of coral reefs and islands providing some of the most spectacular underwater scenery and richest marine life in the world. There are excellent local facilities for scuba diving, snorkeling, windsurfing, and other water sports, as well as for camel trekking on land, and many secluded spots for camping. Beautiful beaches, emerald mangrove lagoons, picturesque wadis, and craggy mountains can easily be explored, although until surprisingly recently this was one of the most remote regions in the world. A journey which used to take days of travel by camel through inhospitable desert now takes a matter of hours by car.

And yet the wilderness you will find will be unspoiled, inhabited by Bedouin and other nomads of the desert, by ibex, hyrax, foxes, reptiles, and birds, and visited by vast flocks of migrating birds using the Red Sea thermals to help them on their way.

Look around at this wilderness. There is life, but it is almost invisible. There are colors, but they are muted and drab. This is an upside-down world, for here the kaleidoscope of life is below the surface. The vivid colors and swirling movement of the coral reefs could not be in greater contrast to the barren land, but a diver, as though looking through a half-submerged mask, can enjoy the best of both.

Geography

The coast of mainland Egypt runs along the Red Sea from Suez down to the border with Sudan. South Sinai's coast dips into the Red Sea from Suez to Ras Mohammed, and north to the Israeli frontier at Taba. The Gulf of Suez separates the mainland from Sinai's western shore, while the Gulf of Aqaba, part of the African rift valley system which runs up to the Dead Sea and the Jordan Valley, lies between eastern Sinai and the Arabian peninsula.

Sinai is drifting away from the African mainland to which it was once joined, and in so doing it is stretching the Gulf of Suez floor between: its maximum depth is only 60 fathoms (110 meters). The Gulf of Aqaba, on the other hand, reaches a depth of 1000 fathoms (1,850 meters) in the latitude of Nuweiba, and so can be numbered among the world's deepest oceans. The Red Sea proper begins at the Straits of Gubal and Tiran, which lie at the mouths of the Gulf of Suez and of Aqaba respectively.

The Red Sea is excessively salt, and the sea bed rich in metalliferous muds which are soon to be mined commercially. Offshore oil is drilled, notably in the Gulf of Suez, and the minerals on shore have been exploited from the turquoise and emerald mines of the ancient Egyptians to the talc, lead, and manganese mines of the present day. The sea's name comes from the sailors of antiquity who visited its shores and called it Mare Rubrum after its mineral-rich red mountains.

The movements of ancient seas have shaped the mountains and the coastline we see today. Ancient granites, gneiss, and schists, worn down by water and time, have been overlaid by sandstones and limestones which can be dated from their fossil deposits to formations beginning in the Cambrian period (600 million–500 million years ago) and continuing up to the Miocene epoch (25 million–10 million years ago). One feature of this process is the raised beaches and uplifted coral rocks, cut through in some places by wadis (dry water courses). During heavy periodic rainfalls water collects in mountain ravines and then gushes down with terrific force, sweeping detritus along with it and in time carving out immense troughs. Effects of these flash floods can be seen all around the coast.

Sometimes in spring, if there has been a spell of rain, the Red Sea deserts turn overnight into meadows carpeted with flowers—purple marguerites, lilies, irises, and numerous others—and the sandy hillocks are lush and green. The plants grow quickly before the sun scorches them, and often it is only a few days before they wither and their seeds are cast to the winds to lie dormant, perhaps for years, until it rains again.

History

"Really, when one looks at these lofty mountains, so arid and rocky," says Henri de Monfreid in his book *Hashish: Smuggling under Sail in the Red Sea*, "one can't help wondering what possessed Moses to bring his people here and make his laws in such a place." Presumably Moses felt safe from the Egyptians, although the pharaohs had a presence in Sinai, exploiting the mineral wealth there as well as in the hills of the mainland coast, since the Middle Kingdom (2040–1640 B.C.). By the Nineteenth Dynasty (1307–1196 B.C.) and the time of Moses, though, they had their hands full in Sinai with rebellious nomadic tribes.

The Egyptians used the Red Sea for maritime commerce from early times, trading with the countries of the Arabian peninsula and Africa, including the mysterious Punt where the great Eighteenth Dynasty queen Hatshepsut (1479–1458 B.C.) sent her famous expedition, for the myrrh and spices needed for temple ceremonies, and for precious woods and ivory. In trade they coexisted with Phoenician traders who traveled from the eastern coast of the Mediterranean. By the first millenium B.C. the Egyptians had established trade links with India. Important overland routes led from Berenice and Kosseir to Thebes; from Suez, through Nakhl, to Palestine and Syria; and from Aqaba to Petra, the stronghold of the Nabateans. Ptolemaic trade was conducted through the ancient mainland ports of Clysma (present-day Suez), Myos Hormos, and Berenice. Meanwhile the Nabateans controlled Sinai until it was annexed by the Roman general Pompey in 64 B.C.

Pilgrim roads along which Moslems traveled to Mecca and, less frequently, Christians to Jerusalem, led from the Nile Valley to Kosseir and from Cairo to Suez and on to Aqaba. It is not surprising that the pilgrims kept to land as much as possible, for sailing was hazardous in the Red Sea. High winds and crosscurrents plagued sailors in the open sea, yet hugging the coast was dangerous because of rocks and coral reefs.

Reynaud de Châtillon, the Crusader lord of Kerak (in western Jordan near the southern Dead Sea), was a menace to pilgrims. In 1182 he had five ships carried by camel from Kerak to the Gulf of Aqaba, where they were assembled and launched. With them he beseiged Pharaoh's Island, then held by Salah el-Din, while

Pharaoh's Island

the rest of his small fleet cruised down the Red Sea, attacking pilgrim and merchant ships. It was this series of raids that prompted the Arab forces to unite and push the Second Crusade back to its final strongholds of Tyre, Antioch, and Tripoli on the Mediterranean.

Prominence in trade in the northern Red Sea then shifted between the entrepôts of Aidhab, Aden, Jeddah, Kosseir, and el-Tor. European exports—from cloth to eastern European slaves—were sent to Arabia and the East, and silks and porcelain from China, cotton from India, African slaves, rice, sugar, wool, precious stones, and Arabian horses were just some of the commodities which passed through the area throughout the period of the Arab caliphates.

As the discovery of new continents opened new trading routes, the Red Sea slipped into decline until the opening of the Suez Canal in 1869, when it was once again established as a major commercial route. The closure of the canal between 1967 and 1975 and Sinai's occupation by the Israelis put much of the Red Sea coast out of bounds to civilians. After the mid-1970s, however, the mainland coast was opened to foreigners as well as to Egyptians, and after the final handover agreement in 1982 tourists from Egypt were able to visit Sinai.

The People of the Red Sea

Sinai and the deserts of Egypt belong to the seminomadic tribes who arrived from Saudi Arabia and from Africa hundreds of years ago. They needed great skill to survive, and their livelihood depended on a knowledge of their environment. Medical skills and religio-magical beliefs were also shaped by the desert. To see a more complete picture of their way of life one should try to visit the hidden pools, farms, and oases known to the Sinai Bedouin, or watch how they find their way on a mountain where one wadi looks much like another to you.

Every part of the desert is patrolled. However remote the area you are passing through, you will see a woman gathering herbs or herding goats. You will hardly catch a glimpse of her beautiful, traditional face covering before she turns away with her back to the road. If your car breaks down or you stop for a picnic, wherever you are, someone will inevitably turn up.

The Sinai Bedouin do not consider themselves Egyptian. It matters little to them who occupies their land, yet their lives are changing rapidly. As land is sold to property developers, the Bedouin see that they too must stake a claim to a patch of land before it all goes up for sale. Their sons are drafted into national service, their daughters attend government schools. They are taking employment—or working for themselves—in the tourist industry, a process started when Sinai was under Israeli control.

The Bedouin deal with the desert in a manner suiting their practical lifestyle but which to us may seem non-environmentalist. In spring, the desert flowers which delight our eyes become precious forage for the herds of black goats which eat everything in sight. Roaming camels graze on the trees as well. In the old days, the tendency of a nomadic people to leave their refuse behind when moving on did little damage to the environment because, being biodegradable, everything would have disappeared or been consumed by the time they came back. In pre-Islamic times a Bedouin poet coming across the traces of a campsite recently abandoned by the tribe of the woman he once loved would be moved to the spontaneous composition of an ode memorializing their romance, the end of which was symbolized by the tent-pegs and blackened hearthstones left behind by her tribe. Nowadays this rubbish consists of tin cans and plastic bags, and in common with the rest of us the Bedouin haven't yet solved the problem of getting rid of it.

The Bedouin sticks to his word and is known to be honest and fair. Remember to show respect for Bedouin property. If you come across an abandoned dwelling or a cache of belongings do not disturb it, for it is probably waiting for the next time its owner passes by. The Bedouin are very polite, and the politeness should always be returned. Their society is egalitarian, and master and servant sit at one table. Bedouin customs can be quite complex to follow, but niceties can easily be learned: coffee should always be drunk, if accepted. If you don't want your cup to be refilled, shake it slightly from side to side.

The Bedouin of the mainland coast are of the Ma'aza tribe, who entered Egypt with the Islamic invaders. From the other direction came a non-Arab people, the Ababde, moving up from the south to settle in the Red Sea hills as far as Kosseir, although over the last hundred and fifty years or so many have moved to the Nile Valley. Traditionally occupied in camel trading, fishing, and herding, their way of life is changing as they settle down, go to school, and seek local employment. Ababde dwellings are structures of wood or metal sheeting. Superficially the Ababde dress much like the Egyptians of the Nile Valley, though they usually go bareheaded, and they tend to heavy bones and features. The Ababde people enjoy offering hospitality; their coffee ritual is slightly different from that of the Bedouin. Traditionally they offer nine small cups: if you can't drink that much, you have to refuse the first one.

Their neighbors the Bishareen also came from Africa, but ventured no further north than Mersa Alam. They keep much more to themselves than do the Ababde, but occasionally you might see a Bishari tribesman in a shop or a taxi. Their appearance is distinctive—a different style of dress, and the hair worn long and wild. The Bishareen are known as great herbalists.

In your dealings with the local people, remember that you are the intruder, and that they were born to a lifestyle that you, with your bubble tent and camping gas, can only begin to appreciate.

The Coral Reefs

Coral used to be something ships got stuck on. Books about the Red Sea are full of dire warnings to sailors. Strabo, writing around 25 B.C., gave the name Sinus Immundus (Foul Bay) to a point which in our day is still part of a stretch "foul with reefs and sunken rocks," as noted in a 1946 British naval intelligence report. The reefs must have been even more beautiful before the craze for shell collecting and the commercial fishing of trochus shells was allowed to despoil them. For the reefs, though, these

opposite: On the track from Ras Abu Galuum to Dahab

were trivial wounds compared with the pollution which was later to come from modern merchant shipping and the oil industry; it is one thing to anchor your sailing vessel to a fine patch of coral, quite another to spill oil over it.

The rule of the Red Sea reefs—enforced by law—is: never take anything out of them, dead or alive. Dead corals and shells break down with time, eventually becoming cemented. The floating larval forms of corals anchor themselves to this hardened limestone, and so each generation adds its improvements to the gardens of the reef. The coral polyps are so fragile that a storm or a cloud of silt can kill whole colonies, so the building process takes many thousands of years, and if the reefs are to be enjoyed in the years to come they must be protected from the ravages of commerce—both that generated by shipping and by tourism.

It is not within the scope of this guide to give comprehensive details of the rich marine life of the Red Sea—there are many good reference books on this subject. Nor is this a sporting handbook. No attempt will be made to give instruction in scuba diving, snorkeling, swimming, or windsurfing. To dive in Egyptian waters, divers must have a valid diver's card or take instruction through one of the courses on offer in several methods—and what better place to learn.

Where should you dive? Fringe reefs, barrier reefs, and patch reefs (see diagram) are all found on or off the Egyptian coast,

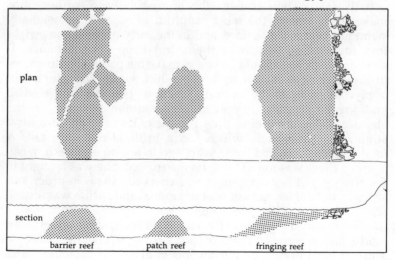

Types of Red Sea reefs

opposite, above: The Apu Hara *near Sharm el-Sheikh;*
below: Assalah, Dahab

though most of the easily accessible fringe reefs are on the eastern coast of Sinai. As a rule, the further south you are, the more big fish—sharks, tuna, and jack fish—you will see. But it is in the Gulf of Aqaba and the Straits of Gubal that the reef builders have been most energetic. Wherever you choose to start, equipment can be hired, but not easily bought: so if you want a mask that fits and a snorkel that doesn't let you down, or a wetsuit that makes you feel human, buy it beforehand and bring it with you. For maximum safety, you should also use your own regulator. Because of the creatures that lurk on the bottom, it cannot be stressed too much that it is inadvisable for anyone—and this includes swimmers and paddlers—to enter the water with nothing on their feet. An old pair of tennis shoes will do, but barefoot is out. Snorkelers should wear boots, and, although many like to snorkel without them, fins give added protection on the soles. Never attempt to swim alone.

Do not touch anything unless you know what it is, and that almost requires the background of a marine biologist. Sharks and barracudas are not such a threat as one might suppose; it's the small things you need to look out for—urchin spines, stonefish, lionfish, and textured cone shells. A wise precaution is to beware of any creature that does not swim away from you—it probably has another means of defense in reserve. Stonefish and scorpion fish lie camouflaged on the rocks; their dorsal spines release a powerful toxin which is painful in the extreme, though not usually fatal. Their cousins the lionfish, whose feathery fins make them among the most beautiful of all fish, occasionally swim just under the surface, and in the early evening come right into the shallows—admire them, but keep your distance. If someone with you should be stung, make the patient lie down, try to lower the circulation by keeping him warm and quiet, and apply hot water to the wound as soon as possible. For jellyfish and fire coral stings, apply diluted ammonia—urine, in the absence of anything else, does the trick. There is no cure for a sting by a cone shell, which has a brilliant-red little tail. A fatal accident occurred some years ago in Sharm el-Sheikh, when a young diver was found lying on the sea bed. She was brought to the surface and her equipment was checked; it was in order, but she was dead. Her wetsuit was unzipped, and inside was a cone shell she had put there for safekeeping.

This is not to put you off visiting this enchanting underwater world, just to warn you to take care. Go ahead, take the plunge—a list of local diving establishments is given for each area, and some of the European operators who bring divers to the Red Sea are listed in the Appendix.

Practical Information

Sinai and the mainland Red Sea coast are connected by a road and air network to Cairo and the Nile Valley, and directly to Europe from where weekly charters fly to Hurghada and Sharm el-Sheikh. Buses run from Cairo or Suéz to all points on the coast, and a bus service runs between Luxor and Hurghada. Ferries operate between Suez or Nuweiba and Aqaba, and intermittently between Hurghada and Sharm el-Sheikh. You can even enter the Red Sea by sailing down through the Suez Canal, although the formalities involved both in passing through the canal and in staying on to enjoy some time in Egypt are aggravating and should not be undertaken without serious forethought. Moses was the first tour leader to the Red Sea, now many operators take diving and adventure tours on boats, camèls, and motorbikes. Information about where to obtain air and bus tickets is given in the Appendix. Other information about transport to and from the area's towns and dive sites may be found in the sections devoted to them in this guide.

All visitors from abroad must register their passports at a police station within seven days of their arrival in Egypt. Make sure that your hotel does this for you, but if you are camping it's your responsibility, and it's all too easy to forget!

If you intend to visit any areas of the coast which require special permits, then do allow plenty of time to organize these. A permit to visit Ras Banas for diving or fishing may be obtained from the Frontiers Administration headquarters in Cairo or from the police station in Hurghada on production of a letter of reference from an official organization such as the Ministry of Tourism. If it is Berenice you want to see, you must make this very clear and insist that your permit is marked "Berenice" and not just "Ras Banas," and this must be arranged at the FA office in Cairo. It might be better not to try to visit Ras Gemsa on your way down the coast, as a permit must be obtained at the police station in Hurghada. As for entering Egypt from Israel through Taba, serious tourists, or divers, will enjoy much more freedom to travel if they obtain a one-month visa beforehand from the Egyptian embassy in their country. Holders of such a visa must make sure that the Taba border guard endorses this with the correct stamp, or they will find themselves in possession of the fourteen-day pass issued to applicants at the border. This pass restricts travel to the Aqaba coast and St. Catherine's, and, keen divers should note, does not extend as far as Ras Mohammed. Note that many Arab countries will not allow admittance to anyone with a Taba stamp in their passports, as it clearly indicates entry from Israel.

Motorists will find roads in excellent condition (barring floods), and with regular gas stations. They should have their vehicles checked before setting out, however, in order to avoid breakdowns. It is forbidden to carry explosive materials such as cans of gasoline and gas cylinders through the Ahmed Hamdi Tunnel leading to Sinai. It is obligatory to keep a fire extinguisher in the car, and to carry your car license and driving license papers. Foreign motorists can drive in Egypt only if they are in possession of an international driving license issued in their own country, or an Egyptian license. An Egyptian driving test takes some time to arrange, so plan ahead and do not leave it until the last moment.

Those driving to the coast from Cairo should take the main Suez road (highway 33). The turning to the Ahmed Hamdi Tunnel for Sinai is 119 kilometers from Cairo. Two roads leave highway 33 for the mainland coast before Suez. A good road also runs from Maadi to the coast at Bir Udeib.

In hotels rated by the Ministry of Tourism with three or more stars you must pay your bill in foreign currency (Egyptian currency may be used if you can produce a receipt showing that you exchanged it in a bank), or with a credit card, unless you are Egyptian or have lived in Egypt for more than five years. Foreign residents should always carry a letter of identification from their employer in order to qualify for payment at the resident's rate. Star ratings, which are not reliable as an indicator of standards, have here been omitted. Instead, hotels have been classified where possible according to their price range. Thus, hotels designated A charge more than LE 125 per night for a double room; those marked B run between LE 50 and LE 125; while those designated C charge under LE 50 for a double room. As a rule single and triple rooms are also available. Unless otherwise stated restaurant prices refer to a table-d'hôte evening meal. Major credit cards are accepted in many large hotels in Sinai.

Sport and relaxation are the order of the day. Winter months and evenings can be cool—take woollens in the winter, cotton jerseys when it starts to get warmer, and cottons for the summer months. Rainfall occurs only between October and April, and even then rarely. July and August are the hottest months, but the prevailing north winds blow away some of the heat. You will need wind shelters most of the year to alleviate the discomfort of these north winds, especially in Dahab and the southern part of Hurghada. Breezes usually drop in April and May, but the weather follows no hard-and-fast rules and what happens one year won't necessarily happen the next. Snorkelers and windsurfers will usually need a wetsuit from November to March, and should wear a shirt in the water to protect them from sunburn during the summer. Except in very cold and windy spells, camping and water sports can be enjoyed all the year round. The Red Sea resorts are the only places in Egypt where shorts are acceptable. Topless sunbathing and public kissing are not.

Medical facilities are limited, although there are clinics in most towns, and hospitals in Hurghada and el-Tor. Mosquitoes are a year-round problem in Hurghada but mosquito coils are unavailable there. Local suntan lotions are very good, but should you get sunburned, vinegar, yogurt, or a cocktail of lemon juice, salt, and oil are handy remedies.

Desert safaris can be arranged in Hurghada and on the Aqaba coast of Sinai. You will be provided with transport and food, but take along a sleeping bag, a swimsuit (for the mountain pools), and treats to supplement the basic menu. You will enjoy this type of activity better if you are physically fit.

Camping is allowed within the limits of a town if no official campsite is provided. It is also allowed anywhere along the coast provided that, for everyone's peace of mind including your own, you observe the following official rules:

1. Ask permission from the nearest police or frontier guard post.
2. Camp at least 100 meters from the beach.
3. Do not enter the water at night without permission.
4. Leave all beaches by sunset if you do not intend to camp.
5. No fires may be lit near the beach, nor flashlights used.

These rules have not been invented at a whim. The problem of smuggling in the gulfs and the Red Sea is almost as old as Egyptian recorded history, and orders are to shoot smugglers on sight.

One final word on shooting: fire away as much as you like in the water—with a camera. No spear guns are allowed in the Red Sea.

1
The Mainland Coast
(Suez to Berenice)

Is it better to dive along the mainland coast, or that of Sinai?
The advantage of the mainland coast is the ease of access from
the Nile Valley—the road from Qena to Port Safaga means that
a holiday can be arranged quite conveniently to incorporate both
the treasures of Luxor and the dive sites of Hurghada. Roads also
cut across the Red Sea mountains to the coast from the Nile
Valley centers of Beni Suef, Minya, and Edfu. Hurghada has a
selection of hotels and holiday villages to suit everyone's
pocket, and more than thirty islands and offshore reefs
compensate for the paucity of fringing coral that is the glory of
Sinai's eastern coast. Although relatively featureless in the
north, the mainland coast becomes more and more beautiful the
further south you go, and if possible the dedicated seeker of
unspoiled open spaces should obtain permission to visit the area
south of Mersa Alam, where white sand beaches and aquamarine
lagoons fringed with mangroves shelter countless species of
migrating birds.

At its northern end, the coast is spattered with oil workings.
Egypt produces an average of 870,000 barrels of oil a day, of
which approximately one-quarter is exported, making oil one of
the country's four biggest sources of revenue together with

tourism, Suez Canal revenues, and remittances from Egyptians working abroad.

The roads are well maintained and gas stations are to be found at regular intervals until Mersa Alam. It would do no harm, though, to carry a can of gasoline as well as a set of tools and a spare fan belt when you set off for the south. Also useful are several packets of cigarettes to pass around to the people who help you when your car does break down.

Take care, especially around the towns: the coast is still riddled with mines hastily laid in the 1967 and 1973 wars. Minefields are usually marked with notices in English (frequently illegible) and with barbed-wire fences, but not always, so keep to well-trodden tracks and to areas where there are clear signs of activity.

Hurghada is a thriving tourist center with several foreign exchange banks, but hardly anyone there takes credit cards—at the moment, only the Giftun Village and the Sheraton do—so make sure that you have sufficient cash or traveler's checks.

Hurghada is linked by air to Cairo, St. Catherine's, and Sharm el-Sheikh.

The Port of Suez

History
Suez, the ancient Ciysma, reached prominence as the trading port of Kolzoum in the seventh century, when Amr ibn el-As reopened the Ptolemaic canal from Bilbeis on the eastern edge of the Delta in order to transport grain for exportation to the

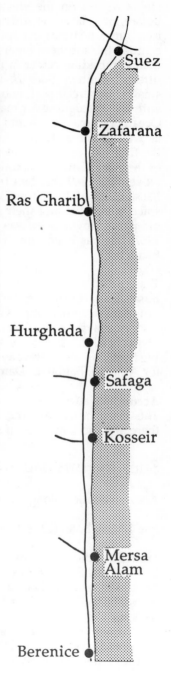

Hejaz region on the western coast of the Arabian peninsula. Before long, however, this canal once again fell into disrepair as Kolzoum's fortunes declined, and by the middle of the eleventh century the southern Sinai port of el-Tor succeeded Kolzoum as the main trading center in the Gulf of Suez. Under the Ottomans, fifteenth-century Suez revived to become a naval as well as a small commercial port, and from here the Turkish fleet struggled with the Portuguese for mastery of the trade routes of the Indian Ocean. The mail route and the P. & O. steamer services to India, as well as the railway line to Cairo, all brought life to Suez in the first half of the nineteenth century, but it was the formation of the Suez Canal Company in 1856 and its official opening on 17 November 1869 that laid the foundation of the modern city and its satellite of Port Tewfik. In spite of this, the ghosts of the spice merchants and their sailing ships haunt the corners of the old part of town. Suez was devastated during the Six-Day War of 1967, but has been rebuilt recently with Arab and World Bank financing.

Transport
Buses leave Cairo regularly for Suez from the East Delta Bus Company terminal at el-Kulali (by the underpass to Shubra), or a service taxi may be taken from behind Ramses railway station at a fare of LE 2. A ferry service departs from Suez at noon on Wednesdays and Saturdays for Aqaba (from Aqaba buses leave for Amman, Baghdad, Damascus, Kuwait, and Saudi Arabia).

Accommodation
The main hotels are the Beau Rivage and the Palazzo Misr; there are also a number of smaller local hotels.

Suez to Hurghada (372 kms)

Accommodation along this route:

Ras Gharib hotel (223.5 kms from Suez)

From Suez the road runs down the west coast of the Gulf of Suez and the Red Sea as far as Berenice.
18 kms: el-Adabiya, a fishing village where the British established a naval harbor during the Second World War.
43 kms: Bir Udeib. If you are coming from Cairo or Maadi (117 kilometers) you will join the coast here. Bedouin houses are spread over the minefields of the plain; one supposes that they, not to mention their camels, learn to tread very

carefully. Water used to be distributed to the Bedouin in oil drums filled on the roadside: now, more hygienically, it is piped. The desert plants along here are especially prolific in spring, when purple marguerites and other flowers are in bloom. One highly poisonous, large-leaved shrub, the *saqarat*, only grows on this part of the coast, being usually found inland in Upper Egypt.

54 kms: The start of the Sumed pipe line.

56 kms: On the left, the sulphur springs and salt marshes of Ain Sokhna, belonging to the same underground system as the springs of Ayun Musa in Sinai and Helwan south of Cairo. The tourist hotel closed in 1967 and has remained so, in spite of having recently been renovated. Any tourist project is in grave risk due to the incidence of uncharted mines laid by both sides during the conflicts.

57.5 kms: Gas station. The road now turns right and hugs the coast, overlooking the ships stacked up as they wait to enter the canal. About eighty ships pass though the canal daily.

60.5 kms: The beach of Ain Sokhna, popular for day campers. Don't stray too far inland from the beach. Unless you have police permission to camp overnight you must leave the beach before sunset, as the coast is patrolled and drug smugglers shot on sight. This stretch of rocky, picturesque coastline continues for another 30 kilometers, and until the road was cut pack camels had to wade round the corners. One can just imagine them, laden with provisions and telegraph poles.

64 kms: Bir Abu Darag: a stretch of rocky swimming beach. Take care along this coast. Only go where you see other people, or where there are tracks or signs of road building. Do not enter fenced areas. Remember that mines can be buried several feet deep or dropped from aircraft and covered only by windblown sand.

On a lighter note, watch for schools of dolphin which in fine weather often come along here for aquarobic practice.

81.5 kms: Wadi Doum, marked by doum palms and a small army camp sheltered by rocks.

90 kms: Abu Darag lighthouse. South of here are a few bays with tempting beaches, but with no indication as to whether or not they are mined. As always, look for signs of activity on the beach, and if you still aren't sure, go somewhere else.

103.5 kms: The road enters a wide sandy plain from which minefield warnings sprout. Alongside runs the old British telegraph line from Suez to Kosseir, the poles standing to attention most of the way to Kosseir without their wires, which have been replaced by radio masts.

123 kms: Ras Zafarana junction. The name, meaning saffron or yellow, is taken from the color of the sandstone rocks. On the right is the road through the Wadi Araba to the monastery of St. Antony (50 kilometers) and on to Beni Suef; on the left the lighthouse, gas station, and a scruffy rest house. If you plan to visit the monasteries of St. Antony and St. Paul remember that they are closed in the afternoons, on Sundays, and during Lent, and that you should not attempt to hike from one to the other without an experienced guide.

131 kms: Mersa Thelmet, a harbor with a stone quay and several dwellings at the foot of Gebel Thelmet (676 meters) which pushes to within three miles of the coast.

148 kms: An excellent paved road to the Monastery of St. Paul (13 kilometers), set in spectacular craggy limestone scenery.

174 kms: Storage tanks at North Elma.

191 kms: After running through a wide gravelly plain which rises slowly in the west and contains numerous wadis, the road touches the sea near a white sand beach which is heavily mined.

199 kms: The October 6 field of the Gulf of Suez Petroleum Company (GUPCO). The shimmering emerald sea has been robbed, along here as in the rest of the gulf, of the vibrant coral reefs that were killed by oil and other pollutants. Now only the dead reefs remain; always regarded as a hazard to ships, they were never explored for their own sake. Writing in the thirties, Henri de Monfreid complained of the metal and concrete refuse of the oil industry and its despoliation of the coastline. *Plus ça change.*

204.5 kms: Ras Abu Bakr oil storage tanks.

217.5 kms: Traffic police checkpoint. In a private car you will probably be waved through, though you may be asked to produce your car or driving license.

223.5 kms: Ras Gharib crossroads, with a gas station and a pleasant little in-and-outdoor cafeteria serving coffee, tea, and light meals. On the right, the road to el-Sheikh Fadl on the east bank of the Nile. On the left, Ras Gharib, which in a short time has developed from an oil company town into an industrial metropolis with dozens of shops, a hospital, two banks, restaurants, a local hotel, a small recreational park, and several service industries. You can also find a post office, tire repair and car mechanics, groceries, a bakery, and an oil company rest house. Some of the older company housing is clustered down by the harbor, while newer dwellings are on the outskirts.

229 kms: Southern fork to Ras Gharib. The main road continues to Ras Shukheir along a causeway that separates the sea from the Mallaha plain, an expanse of quicksand sodden with salt water under a crusty surface. Gebel Gharib dominates the distant skyline.

248 kms: The GUPCO airport, servicing the oil fields at Ras Shukheir.

255 kms: Ras Shukheir, the headquarters of GUPCO, with clusters of oil rigs, rig tenders, and tanks overlooking a crystal green bay.

From Ras Shukheir the road runs SSE while the coast noses out and round Gebel Zeit (Mountain of Oil, 460 meters high), a red mountain fringed with old reefs and raised beaches. Oil seeps naturally from its flanks—hence its name. Below the tip of the nose, at Zeituna, Geziret Ghanim marks the northern end of the Straits of Gubal. On the right-hand side are the Mallaha hills.

295 kms: The road around Zeit Bay to Gebel Zeit. You can see the Zeituna oil tanks perched on the edge of the cape.

307 kms: The road forks left to the Bahar North East field.

313 kms: The road to Ras Gemsa, a bare limestone promontory whose two long fingers curl around Gemsa Bay. About 5 kilometers along the sand track is a camel police station; to go beyond it you will need a permit from the Military Intelligence Office in Hurghada. You will find wonderful, secluded nooks and crannies for camping, which is why it is so heavily patrolled for drug smuggling. At the far point are the ruins of a port and of the first oil well in Egypt, bored in 1908, and of the later phosphate mines, extensively damaged during the 1967 war. There are still some oil workings on the south side.

Gebel Esh looms ahead, almost reaching the road at 332 kilometers.

352 kms: The coastal range comes to a sudden end with Gebel Abu Shar el-Qibli. Nearby was the Ptolemaic port of Myos Hormos, of which nothing now remains; whatever existed of the harbor of Abu Shar, which is marked on many maps though information about it is limited, may have similarly disappeared under silt and sand. A track (for four-wheel-drive vehicles only) runs round the edge of the plain ahead to the old Roman porphyry quarries at Mons Porphyrites (Gebel Abu Dukhan).

366 kms: Traffic police checkpoint and the "Youth and Families Camp" for Egyptian youth organizations.

367 kms: Museum of Marine Biology (aquarium). No entrance fee. The museum is in the yellow building at the end of the cul-de-sac. It is a theater of the grotesque, with a collection of mounted sharks, rays, and dugongs, and a giant leatherback turtle nailed to the wall. Behind the museum, at the end of the jetty, reef fishes and other creatures including crabs and Spanish dancers are kept, for the benefit of the nonswimming public, in small glass tanks, most of them sleeping and, one hopes, dreaming of other waters. Behind these sheds, a couple of turtles swim languidly in large tanks walled off from the sea, but filled with sea water which rises with the tide.

370 kms: Hurghada by-pass.

372 kms: The mosque and central square of Hurghada.

Hurghada

Development of the town

In a part of the world where towns are thousands of years old, here is one founded by the British in 1909. About two hundred British and Italian mining engineers working for the Shell company, with their families, servants, and Egyptian mining employees, settled in what is still the city center, sometimes erroneously called New Hurghada (there is no Old Hurghada). Local tribesmen had given the area the name Ghardaqa, after the prickly, yellow-leaved shrub which grows here in abundance. Major C. S. Jarvis, onetime governor of Sinai, tells in his book *Three Deserts* how the name came to be changed: "The Anglo–Egyptian oil fields on the Gulf of Suez are at a place named after this shrub, but the mining engineers, after suffering from sore throats for some time, rechristened the spot Hurghada, which is sufficiently near to the correct name to be recognizable and can be correctly pronounced by everybody, providing there is no difficulty about sounding the aspirate."

Conditions in the new settlement must have been very harsh. Apart from some wells in the mountains the area had no water, which had to be brought by ship from Suez. Nevertheless the engineers stayed and drilled their oil wells (production started in 1914) and built a British and an Italian school. During the following decade or so some fishing families from Saudi Arabia, from Saudi stock in Sinai, and from Kosseir settled beside the harbor in Sigalla (four kilometers down the road). These few Arab families formed a close-knit community, and their houses, now sadly dilapidated, can still be seen lining the beach along the Shohada Road, between the two mosques of Sigalla. The Frontiers Administration camp and barracks were also built near the harbor. A boat-building industry was established which today thrives on the building of boats to take divers out to the reefs.

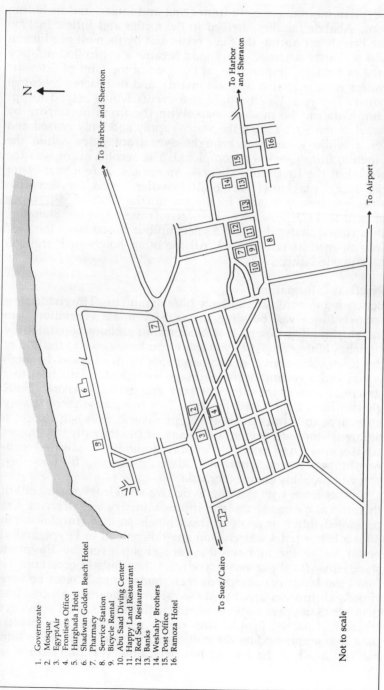

N

To Harbor and Sheraton

To Harbor
and Sheraton

To Airport

To Suez/Cairo

Hurghada

Not to scale

1. Governorate
2. Mosque
3. EgyptAir
4. Frontiers Office
5. Hurghada Hotel
6. Shadwan Golden Beach Hotel
7. Pharmacy
8. Service Station
9. Bicycle Rental
10. Abu Saad Diving Center
11. Happy Land Restaurant
12. Red Sea Restaurant
13. Banks
14. Weshahy Brothers
15. Post Office
16. Ramoza Hotel

Egyptian migrants, mostly from Qena and Luxor, and including some Ababde families, arrived in the forties and fifties. In 1956 the British left during the Suez crisis, but by then oil production had seriously declined. Hurghada became a controlled military area of strategic importance, at the gate of the Gulf of Suez; its waters were patrolled by coast guards, and its beaches by camel police. The year 1967 brought two events which helped to put Hurghada on the modern map. With the first, the seizure by Israel of the Suez Canal, the water supply suddenly ceased and for a while water was brought over from Aden while the pipeline from Qena was completed. The second event was the arrival of the first scuba divers—Americans. A few years later the Hurghada Hotel was built (smaller hotels for Egyptian workers already existed in the town), the Club Méditerranée opened in 1977 (now owned by Misr Travel), and the Sheraton, constructed under different ownership but closed since the 1967 war, opened at last in 1979. All the other hotels in Hurghada have opened since 1982.

Practical information

Between an azure sea and hazy blue mountains, Hurghada now sprawls like a vast building site with even less vegetation than the surrounding desert. It is broken into sections separated by stretches of desert; just as you think you have come to the end of the town, you arrive at another patch of it. Plagued by high winds and a chronic water shortage, Hurghada plays host to a stream of disappointed backpackers, and even the smarter hotel ghettos have their bored inmates. This is because there is very little here to attract anyone except divers, who can expect a different story altogether, and many of the tour dive operators advise nondiving partners to stay at home. Dedicated sun-worshippers should ignore this advice; if this will fill your day, you will probably enjoy Hurghada.

In this town with nothing to do (we shall leave divers out of this for a moment) an ambitious Ministry of Tourism has promoted thirty or so new, small hotels so that Hurghada can offer a better hotel service than any other town in Egypt, and at better value for money—they are cheap even by Egyptian standards—for those very travelers it then fails to entertain. To fulfill the Ministry's standards these budget hotels must be very clean and provide fans, hot showers, and cafeterias. All cost less than LE 15 per person; none accept credit cards. Aimed at budget travelers (that is, people who travel with their own towels) they also accommodate the cost-conscious end of the dive tour market. Most of the budget travelers, however, don't come to

Hurghada to dive, and a snorkeling trip to Giftun Island will be as much as most can afford.

Tourism increased sixfold among Egyptians in the years 1980 to 1986, and threefold for foreign tourists, bringing the numbers of each up to well over thirty thousand a year. The Red Sea Governorate, which controls the area between Ras Zafarana and Mersa Alam, plans a hotel riviera from Hurghada to Port Safaga, and much of this is already underway. As well as scuba diving, almost all of which is offshore, much of the emphasis is on fishing, windsurfing, or just being jolly (see Giftun Village). Nevertheless pharaonic, Roman, Coptic, and Islamic remains are to be found along the coast, and the Tourist Office in Governorate House can arrange guided excursions to sites which include the white granite quarries of Mons Claudianus and the porphyry mines at Gebel Abu Dukhan at a cost of U.S. $35 per person, which includes lunch.

Conservation is a major issue here. In the desert, deer and foxes; in the sea, dolphins, dugongs, turtles, manta rays, and reef fishes are protected, and no shells or corals may be taken from the water. Sadly, some shops in Hurghada do deal in shells and other dead marine creatures, but they are prohibited from replenishing their stock with animals taken after the conservation laws came into force. Tourists are the main culprits. They buy these "souvenirs," and they often insist on collecting them themselves on boat trips. Boat captains are not permitted to allow shells or corals to be brought aboard and may lose their license if they do, so it is unfair to compromise your captain.

The beaches around Hurghada are spoiled by harbor waste, but it is planned to clean up the northern beach (near the Hurghada Hotel) by 1990. There is a public beach south of the Sheraton, but it has no toilet or changing facilities. However for a charge of LE 5 you may use any of the holiday village beaches, the best of which is the Sheraton.

Several shops are grouped in the center of town. Post cards and souvenirs can be bought at the Black Horse or the Younis Bazaar or in a new parade of shops near the souk; there are several shops where you can rent or buy snorkeling equipment, several pharmacies, a new post office, and banks. Towards Sigalla is Stop Shop, an upmarket furniture and gift store, and next door the Stop Shop Laundry and Dry Cleaning.

Local transport

Minibuses run between the town center and Sigalla. The cost is 10 piasters—pay the driver as you get off.

The mosque in central Hurghada

Public buses run hourly between the town center and el-Samaka Village, stopping at hotels en route and at Sigalla. Fare to el-Samaka: 25 piasters.

Taxi drivers know all the hotels and restaurants, and can usually answer your questions. The fare from Sigalla to the souk area is LE 1, to the central mosque LE 2, and to the holiday villages or the Marine Sports Club LE 5. Sharing a service taxi to the Marine Sports Club is only 50 piasters. Taxis can be arranged to Luxor or to St. Catherine's—your hotel will help negotiate the fare.

Bikes may be hired from two shops in the city center, and one in Sigalla.

Car journeys from Cairo take six to seven hours, from Luxor four hours.

Private yachts should not be brought to Hurghada unless you have the infinite patience needed to obtain permission to move in and out of the harbor or to buy diesel fuel and supplies. If you have any problems go directly to the Tourist Administration Office in Governorate House, who will try to help you.

Dive centers
The diving in Hurghada is stupendous and includes one of the most outstanding sites in the world, **Careless Reef**, a table 20 meters below the surface teeming with marine life of every kind. Almost all the diving in Hurghada is offshore; only the Moon Valley and Megawish have coral of their own. For this reason diving packages have to be arranged with a dive center. These can be from as short as a day to as long as a month or more, but choose carefully in order to find a center that suits your needs.
   If you want to dive seriously and visit the best reefs in Hurghada, then your holiday should be arranged as such. It has to be stressed that most of the diving is organized by tour operators, the majority from West Germany. A short list of operators is given in the Appendix. Companies vary in policy: some bring tours to be accommodated by local diving agencies, others are brought out by the agencies themselves. Several agencies cater to divers who come in "from the street," some, such as SUBEX, do so only in the low season when they have vacancies, and others, such as Rudi Kneip, do not do so at all.
   Divers who have hired or brought along their own equipment can accompany the snorkeling boats to **Giftun Island**. Like the surrounding islands, Giftun is a barren coral island inhabited by crabs and visited by birds and motorboats. It has a long, white

sand beach with small patches of coral and a variety of reef fish, an idyllic place to sunbathe, snorkel, or swim. A trip to Giftun includes a visit to an offshore site and a fish barbecue lunch followed by an hour or two on the island.

Dive centers are to be found in all the holiday villages and at one or two other hotels, and can be referred to under that section. In addition, the following dive centers should be of assistance to independent divers:

Abu Saad+SUBEX: With its head office in Switzerland, SUBEX mainly handles tours from Europe, and reservations must be made during the high season from September to April. The full range of equipment can be hired to divers taking a boat package. Inexperienced divers are accepted and courses taken by arrangement. A typical day excursion is SFr 62 per day (or equivalent in Egyptian pounds or dollars) including boat travel, two dives, tanks, weight belt, taxes, permits, and lunch. Guests are accommodated in the clubhouse, which has a very fine bar. Divers not used to the style might find diving in large groups, a method favored by the Swiss and the Italians, rather off-putting. The SUBEX office is in Sigalla, while Abu Saad has another office in the center of town, near the Happy Land restaurant. Abu Saad+SUBEX, Hurghada Port, Red Sea. Telephone: (062) 440435.

Dolphin Aqua Centre: With prices for courses and boat trips similar to Weshahy's (see below), Dolphin also offers a PADI introductory dive for LE 100. Shark-observation cruises go to the Brothers Islands opposite Kosseir, and to virgin territory even further south. Dolphin Aqua Centre, Hurghada, Red Sea. Telephone: (062) 440012.

Hani Minyawi Dive Co.: Largely a tour operator for groups from the United States (where it has an office in Detroit), the company also arranges dive packages and accommodation for individuals with PADI, NAUI, and MEDIA courses. A two-dive shore excursion is LE 75, a boat excursion LE 85, an open-water course LE 200 plus U.S. $100 inclusive. No snorkeling. Hani Minyawi Dive Co., Hurghada, Red Sea. Telephone: (062) 440780. Detroit office telephone: 313-851-4008.

Selim Dive Centre: Near the old bus station in the town center, Selim offers two-dive boat trips for experienced divers only for LE 70, LE 45 for one dive, and snorkeling trips for LE 15 including mask, snorkel, fins, and lunch. Selim Dive Centre, Hurghada, Red Sea. Telephone: (062) 440623.

Weshahy Brothers: Ashraf and Ayman run the dive center from an office in the street next to the new post office in the town center. They offer PADI and MEDIA courses, PADI up to assistant instructor level. They also offer full equipment hire. A two-dive boat trip including tanks, weights, and guide is LE 80. An open-water course is LE 350 plus U.S. $50 for the certificate of qualification, including all equipment, a log book, and dive table. Discounts can be made for groups, and hotel accommodation found for groups and individuals. Other water sports include windsurfing, water-skiing, and glass-bottomed boat trips (all by arrangement with the Sheraton Hotel) and fishing (by arrangement with local fishermen). Four- to ten-day dive cruises visit dive sites in the Gulf of Aqaba. Weshahy Brothers, Hurghada, Red Sea. Telephone: (062) 440280.

All the dive centers use the Sheraton telex: 92750 UN.

The snorkeling boats and many of the dive boats leave from the Marine Sports Club, which is past Sigalla, just before the el-Samaka Hotel at 383.5 kilometers from Suez.

A clinic for hyperbolic medicine and diving maladies, with a decompression chamber, is installed at Megawish.

Desert safaris
Abdel Aziz organizes safaris into the mountains with Bedouin guides. An excursion is U.S. $35 for one full day, U.S. $120 for two, including overnight camping. Contact Abdel Aziz at the Abu Ramada hotel, telephone: (062) 440617/440618, or at the Tourist Information Office in Governorate House.

Accommodation
The following is a selection of hotels in or near the town center. Ask at your hotel for information on diving, snorkeling, fishing, or safari trips; air, bus, and ferry times; taxi bookings; and any other service you may require such as laundry or dry cleaning.

Hotels with a Ministry of Tourism rating of three or more stars charge a supplementary rate to foreign tourists. Most of these hotels accommodate foreign residents in Egypt at the Egyptian rate, while a few do not pass the extra tax on to the customer.

All hotels in the Hurghada area use the Sheraton telex: 92750 UN. Only the Sheraton and the Giftun accept credit cards.

(B) Shadwan Golden Beach: On the north beach, unsuitable for swimming but due to be cleaned in 1990, the Shadwan has a spacious swimming pool and sunbathing area, a popular discotheque, and an ice cream parlor, and arranges snorkeling and

diving excursions. Foreign residents are expected to pay the tourist rate, almost double that of Egyptians. No credit cards.

(C) Abu Ramada: A pleasant hotel with friendly staff, this is the base for Aziz Safaris. Room service. Some rooms have private bathrooms. No credit cards. Reservations: Abu Ramada Hotel, Hurghada, Red Sea. Telephone: (062) 440617/440618.

(C) Gobal: The Gobal has a pleasant lobby and cafeteria, and 30 well-furnished rooms, some with balconies, including 4 triples and 7 singles. Tours are organized including diving and snorkeling trips and desert safaris. Each floor has its own lounge. The rooftop garden has a sunbathing area. Dinner is LE 4.50. No credit cards. Reservations: Gobal Hotel, Hurghada, Red Sea. Telephone: (062) 440623.

(C) Hurghada Hotel: Next to the Shadwan Hotel on the north beach, the hotel is friendly and informal, with a pleasant garden. The prefabricated chalets are now looking rather worn, but all have bathrooms. Arrangements can be made here for snorkeling and diving trips. No credit cards. Reservations: Hurghada Hotel, Hurghada, Red Sea. Telephone: (062) 440393.

(C) Luxor Tourist Flats: Five triple rooms with use of a communal kitchen and shower rooms, LE 3 per person. No credit cards. Just next door to the Younis Bazaar.

(C) New Mino: Sixteen rooms divided into family flats, each with a kitchen and bathroom. No credit cards. Reservations: New Mino Hotel, Hurghada, Red Sea. Telephone: (062) 440105.

(C) Ramoza: Centrally located, the Ramoza is a comfortable, friendly hotel with a top-floor cafeteria and roof-garden bar. The *Ramozas I, II,* and *III,* under the direction of Captain Hassan, take snorkelers to Giftun Island for LE 15 including a fish barbecue, or LE 17 with the hire of mask, fins, and snorkel. Rooms with a private bath are only slightly more than those without, with breakfast included. No credit cards. Reservations: Ramoza Hotel, Hurghada, Red Sea. Telephone: (062) 440608.

Restaurants
The following are good, clean restaurants, mostly specializing in sea food, and costing less than LE 10 per head for a full lunch or dinner.

Aly Baba: Dry, but what it lacks in alcohol it makes up for in atmosphere. Excellent fish.

Baron: Shish kebab and kofta, cheap and delicious.

Gobal: On the ground floor of the Gobal Hotel, recommended for plain, well-cooked food, especially fish. The Swedish pine walls are clear of dust-gathering fishing bric-a-brac.

Happy Land: Outdoor and indoor sections, overdecorated but very lively, with superb food and a wider-than-usual menu. Try the calamari pizza and the wonderful frothy lemonade. Often full in the evenings, but less busy at lunchtime.

Red Sea: Under the same ownership as the Abu Nawas Hotel, the food is good but the interior decor rather dreary. Weather permitting, eat on the roof which is very pleasant. The lentil soup is delicious. Service can be rather off-hand.

Weshahy: Popular restaurant which plays the latest pop music. In addition to lunch and dinner try the excellent breakfast with banana milk shake or fresh orange juice.

Hurghada to Port Safaga (61 kms)

Accommodation along this route:

Abu Nawas Hotel (in Sigalla)
Sherry Hotel (376.5 kms from Suez)
Moon Valley (378.5 kms)
Sheraton Hotel (380.5 kms)
Mashrabeya (381.5 kms)
Giftun Village (382.5 kms)
Youth Hostel (382.5 kms)
El-Samaka Village (384 kms)
Princess Village (384 kms)
Hor Palace (384.5 kms)
Megawish (387 kms)
Jasmine Village (391.5 kms)
Sealand Village (417 kms)
Sun Beach Camping (429 kms)

Diving facilities along this route:

Rudi Kneip (see Appendix)
SUBEX (in Sigalla)
Scuba-Doo (378 kms from Suez)

Dive sites along this route:

Moon Valley (378.5 kms from Suez)
Megawish (387 kms)
Sharm el-Naga (417 kms)

376 kms from Suez: **Sigalla**, the harbor area. An ice plant is north
of the boat yards in a yellow building. In Sigalla are to be
found the hospital, the Abu Nawas Hotel, the SUBEX and
Rudi Kneip dive centers, and the old fishermen's houses, with
the oldest on the beach itself. On the Sheraton road just
beyond the harbor area is an estate of terraced bungalows that
look rather like tourist cottages. This is a rehousing scheme
for the fishermen, but not very popular as the new houses are
considered too small.

To reach the Sheraton Hotel and the tourist villages
situated on the Port Safaga road, take the road from the
harbor circle which leads past the hospital.

Accommodation

(B) *Sherry*: A five-minute walk from Sigalla on the Sheraton
road, the Sherry is a block away from the beach on the right-
hand side of the road. Finished to a high standard and opened in
January 1988, it has 25 rooms and family suites equipped with
telephone and room service, TV, sound system, and air
conditioning. The top-floor restaurant looks over the surrounding
desert and towards the sea. Discotheque, but as yet no shops or
swimming pool. Diving for both experienced and inexperienced
divers, snorkeling, fishing, and desert safari trips are all
organized through agencies outside the hotel. Dinner is LE 11.40.
No credit cards. Reservations: Sherry Hotel, Sheraton–
Hurghada Road, Hurghada, Red Sea. Cairo telephone:
850586/866257.
(C) *Abu Nawas*: A stylish little hotel with an open-air bar and
restaurant, a warm atmosphere, and simple, tasteful decoration.
The Abu Nawas is located in a quieter area near the sea, and is
more charming than some of the "boxes" in town. Service is
willing, but erratic: there may be Mozart with breakfast, or no
breakfast at all. Gathering point for old salts from the harbor.

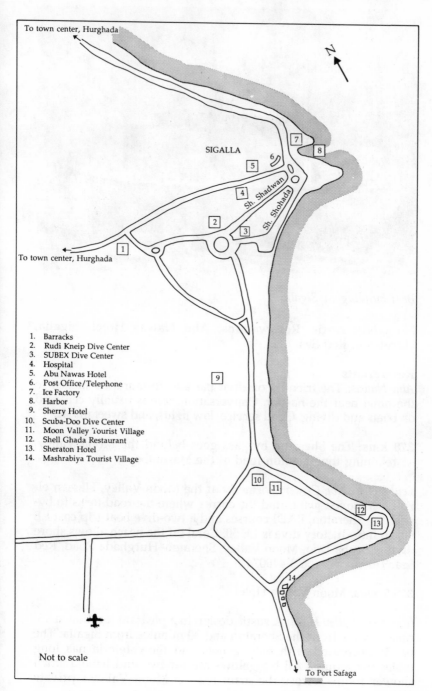

To town center, Hurghada

SIGALLA

To town center, Hurghada

Sh. Shadwan

Sh. Shohada

1. Barracks
2. Rudi Kneip Dive Center
3. SUBEX Dive Center
4. Hospital
5. Abu Nawas Hotel
6. Post Office/Telephone
7. Ice Factory
8. Harbor
9. Sherry Hotel
10. Scuba-Doo Dive Center
11. Moon Valley Tourist Village
12. Shell Ghada Restaurant
13. Sheraton Hotel
14. Mashrabiya Tourist Village

Not to scale

To Port Safaga

Sigalla

Boat-building in Sigalla

No credit cards. Reservations: Abu Nawas Hotel, Sigalla, Hurghada, Red Sea.

Restaurants
Abu Nawas: The friendly outdoor bar and restaurant attached to the hotel near the harbor. Conversation here is usually centered on boats and diving. Good service, low lights, and sweet music.

378 kms: The Sheraton by-pass goes behind the Moon Valley, rejoining the Sheraton road at the Mashrabeya.

Scuba-Doo Dive Center: Formerly at the Moon Valley, Hassan el-Foli has moved just round the corner where the road forks to by-pass the Sheraton. PADI courses and a two-dive boat trip cost LE 90, an introductory dive is LE 50. Coral off the beach allows shore diving. Scuba-Doo, Moon Valley, Sheraton–Hurghada Road, Red Sea. Telephone: (062) 440074.

378.5 kms: Moon Valley Hotel.

(C) Moon Valley Hotel: A rustic design in a pleasant location, a 15-minute walk from the Sheraton and 30 minutes from Sigalla. The bar is decorated with fishing nets and the cafeteria has long tables for groups. All bungalows are for two and have a small shower room. Across the main road is Moon Valley's private

beach which has a fringing-coral reef; diving is by arrangement with Scuba-Doo, next door to the hotel. Dinner is LE 5. No credit cards. Reservations: Moon Valley Hotel, Sheraton–Hurghada Road, Hurghada, Red Sea. Telephone: (062) 440074.

380 kms: Shell Ghada restaurant.
380.5 kms: Sheraton Hotel.

(A) Sheraton Hotel: Built in 1964 by EGOTH (Egyptian Organization for Tourism and Hotels), it was closed in 1967, to be reopened in 1979 as a Sheraton hotel. Situated on the tip of the bay, it has casuarina-fringed gardens ingeniously fed by the hotel's waste water. There are three bars, the nicest one in the central open-air atrium. The hotel and the service can be disorganized, but the beach (open to nonresidents for LE 5) and the pool are certainly gorgeous, although there is no coral off the beach. Water sports include windsurfing, water-skiing, glass-bottomed boat trips, fishing, and snorkeling expeditions. With prior notice diving arrangements can be made with nearby dive centers. Foreign residents are charged the tourist rate. Chalet rooms are cheaper than those in the main building, and cabanas even less. Major credit cards are accepted. Reservations: Hurghada Sheraton Hotel, Hurghada, Red Sea. Telephone: (062) 440779/440604. Telex: 92750 SHRGA UN. Cairo office: P.O. Box 125, Orman Street, Giza. Telephone: 3488215/3485571. Telex: 22761/93355 SHEBO UN.

381 kms: Sheraton by-pass rejoins the road from the Sheraton.
381.5 kms: Mashrabeya Hotel.

(A) Mashrabeya Hotel: Splendid two-story villa accommodation opened in the summer of 1988 with a swimming pool, squash and tennis courts, croquet lawn, water-skiing, windsurfing, snorkeling trips, and a fully-equipped dive center. For the evenings there are three bars and—believe it or not—a glass-bottomed disco (over imported coral, as there is none off the beach). Reservations: Mashrabeya Hotel, Hurghada, Red Sea. Telephone: (062) 441190/441602/441603. Cairo reservations: AMCON Group, 32 el-Misaha Street, Dokki. Telephone: 3600736/3485381. Telex: 20021 AMCON UN.

Just past the Mashrabeya is the public beach, which has the advantage of being free though there are no changing or toilet facilities.

382.5 kms: Giftun Village.

(B) Giftun Village: The Giftun, a luxurious village of Spanish-style whitewashed bungalows, offers a complete holiday. There is a pleasant beach with wind shelters and a bar, a swimming pool, tennis and squash courts, a playground, a fitness room, and handball, aerobics, and beach games organized by the hyperactive Animation Team. The largest windsurfing school in the Middle East runs step-courses of three hours each at DM 45 (or equivalent in dollars or Egyptian pounds) per course; with hire of day-glo wetsuits and harness each at DM 80 a day, or DM 2 an hour. Hire of a sailboard is DM 16 for an hour, DM 50 for a day. The diving center offers PADI, Vit., VOST, VDTL, and CMAS courses, with a five- to six-day course at DM 280. A two-dive boat trip is DM 65. Snorkeling trips (LE 5 for hire of mask, fins, and snorkel) are run from the Aquacentre; so is a glass-bottomed boat and two- to three-day deep-sea fishing trips. Day trips to Luxor can be arranged through affiliated travel agents. A discotheque with an oriental dancer is held outdoors in summer, indoors in winter. There are several shops and an information center, and buses leave for Hurghada town at 10:00 A.M. and 5:00 P.M., returning at 12:00 P.M. and 7:00 P.M. American Express and Visa cards are accepted. The buffet dinner is LE 12. The high season is permanent, so advance booking is necessary. Reservations: Clubhotel Giftun Village, Hurghada, Red Sea. Telephone: (062) 440665/441009. Fax: (062) 440666. Telex: 23629 GIFTO UN. Cairo office: Victoria Hotel, 66 Gomhoria Street. Telephone: 910771/918038/918766/918869. Telex: 92914 VICTO UN.

There is a bright and elegant new youth hostel opposite the Giftun.

383.5 kms: Marine Sports Club, departure point for the snorkeling boats and many of the dive boats. Club entrance is 50 piasters, for which you can use the facilities: garden, cafeteria, and shop. Accommodation is available at LE 30 for a double room. The entrance fee is automatically included in snorkeling packages.

384 kms: Princess and el-Samaka Villages.

(A) Princess Village: The Princess, which opened in December 1987, is arranged much like a real village with low-rise apartments grouped around small squares. Only the villas overlook the sea. There is a long swimming pool, and the good beach has windscreens and a bar; an artificial lagoon makes it very safe for swimming. There is some coral off the beach. A small shop sells groceries, wine, and post cards, and a foreign-exchange facility is

provided. The rooms and apartments all have kitchenettes for preparing light meals which makes it an ideal place to bring a family. Accommodation is of three types: studio apartments, one-bedroom apartments with sofa beds (sleeping up to six), and two-story villas. The dive center offers full equipment hire and PADI courses, snorkeling, and windsurfing. Dinner is LE 15. No credit cards. Cairo reservations: 14 Marashly Street, Zamalek. Telephone: Cairo 3401239. Telex: 23740.

(B) el-Samaka Holiday Village: Very jolly in the evening when attention is focused on the disco and the diminutive oriental dancer Mona Sherif. Accommodation is in rather plain bungalows. There are three bars, a foreign-exchange facility, a tennis court, volleyball, and table tennis. The beach is rather ordinary; the lagoon is suitable for swimming or windsurfing (LE 13 an hour). The dive center has a full range of equipment for hire, and offers an open-water course for LE 264. No credit cards. Reservations: el-Samaka Holiday Village, Hurghada, Red Sea. Telephone: (062) 40227. Cairo reservations: Zoser, 54 Nazih Khalifa Street, Heliopolis. Telephone: Cairo 2580678/2590509.

384.5 kms: Hor Palace.

(A) Hor Palace: Luxury white stone bungalows in an otherwise bleak part of the bay. The beach is on a 150 meter causeway jutting into the sea on the edge of the tide, leading to a small marina. The restaurant on the beach, behind a garden of hollyhocks, serves French and local food at LE 12.50 for the table d'hôte menu. The village has a summer discotheque, outdoor and indoor bar, shops, windsurfing, and plans for sailing, but no pool as yet. A boat takes fishing trips and snorkeling–barbecue trips to Giftun Island. Diving is organized through Abu Saad+SUBEX or Dolphin. No credit cards. Foreign residents are charged the tourist supplement. Reservations: Hor Palace, Hurghada, Red Sea. Telephone: (062) 441710/440603. Cairo office: Telephone: 3410358.

387 kms: Megawish.

(A) Megawish (Umm 'Agawish): At the windy end of Hurghada which resembles a bleak lunar landscape in bad weather, the village was established by the Club Méditerranée and taken over by Misr Travel in November 1987, though the French management happily remained. The activities on offer include fishing, water-skiing, tennis, table tennis, basketball, volleyball, archery, windsurfing, diving, and snorkeling. The

dive center offers boat diving, equipment hire, and instruction. For relaxation there is a swimming pool, a discotheque, and show. Every meal is an open buffet. All foreign residents should bring a letter of identification from their company or employer in order to qualify for payment at the Egyptian rate. Reservations: Misr–Sinai Travel Co., Megawish, Hurghada, Red Sea. Telephone: (062) 440759. Cairo reservations: Misr Travel, P.O. Box 1000, 1 Talaat Harb Street, Cairo. Tel: 3930077/ 3930010/3930063. Fax: 3924440. Telex: 20771/22777.

389 kms: Traffic police checkpoint.
391.5 kms: Jasmine Village.

(B) Jasmine Village: 360 rooms, two restaurants, night club, gymnasium, squash and tennis courts. Cairo reservations: 18 Borsa Street, Tewfiqiyya. Telephone: 744447/777238. Fax: 760159.

408.5 kms: A sandy bay sheltered by sloping cliffs; the very sandy approach makes it accessible only to four-wheel-drive vehicles.
417 kms: Sealand Village at the southern end of Sharm el-Naga, a wide bay that provides some of the best shore diving on the coast. The weather here is pleasant, and usually less windy than in the Megawish area; beside the village is a small bay with a pretty coral garden and a small beach sheltered from the north winds.

(B) Sealand Village: Sealand opened in 1987 and provides accommodation in comfortably furnished tents. The fully-equipped dive center offers shore or boat dives in one- to eleven-day diving packages, PADI courses, equipment hire, snorkeling, and windsurfing. Night dives can be made in safety from the beach. Many people will find the accommodation overpriced for a tent with a communal bathroom, but the management claims that the remoteness of their location justifies the price. Discounts are offered to groups. The set dinner is LE 15. No credit cards. Reservations: Sealand, 47 Falaki Street, Cairo. Telephone: 3545060/3545576. Telex: 94109 SEENA UN.

Sealand is 7 kilometers from the main road along a sandy track. You will find camping sites sheltered by low sand dunes if you turn left when you reach the coast, instead of going south to the village, as long as you obtain permission from the nearby coast guards.

On the way to Port Safaga rows of jagged mountains fringe the coastline, here unspoilt by the oil paraphernalia that de Monfreid complained about so bitterly.

429 kms: Sun Beach Camping.

Sun Beach Camping, with accommodation either in rooms (LE 20 for a double room, with dinner and breakfast) or you may pitch your own tent (LE 2 per person). Snorkeling trips are offered (LE 10 including the boat trip, equipment, and lunch). The cafeteria serves dinner at LE 6. Sun Beach is clean, friendly, and provides a safe, convenient place to camp.

Next door to Sun Beach is Mena Ville, a new project.

433 kms: The right fork in the road is the Qena road, the left goes into Port Safaga.

Port Safaga

In a huge bay with Safaga Island stretching across the horizon, this agreeable little town is the second port of Egypt, the depot of grain imported from Australia, Canada, and the United States and of Australian aluminum destined for the aluminum plant at Nag' Hammadi. Rows of grain silos stand alongside the port, and an occasional cruise liner waits while its passengers visit Luxor for the day. In town are a gas station, post office, and telephone office, a local cinema, fruit and vegetable markets, and several stores. Diving facilities are limited.

Accommodation

(C) Maka Hotel: Opposite the gas station in the center of town, the Maka has 55 rooms. Those double rooms with private bath are better than those without, as the communal bathrooms could be improved. Next-door is an à la carte but dry restaurant: breakfast is LE 1, lunch LE 3.50, dinner LE 3.

(C) El-Okby Village: Pink sugar-icing tourist village facing the sea, with a view of the port. There are family apartments with a kitchen and bathroom sleeping four to five, and double rooms, several of which have private bathrooms. El-Okby has a large terrace area, a sea-water swimming pool, a pleasant restaurant, and a disco bar. The village has two boats for fishing, diving,

and snorkeling trips, and a dive center under German direction. Reservations: El-Okby Village, Port Safaga, Red Sea. Telephone: Port Safaga 1310.

The Safaga Hotel and the new el-Safa el-Marwa Hotel are not open as this book goes to press.

Restaurant
The Hassan Hussein fish restaurant on the main road just past the port serves fish, calamari, and salad in ample portions at LE 6.

Port Safaga to Kosseir (83 kms)

Accommodation along this route:

Tourist village near Old Kosseir (510 kms from Suez)

As you leave Port Safaga you will see running beside the road the disused narrow-gauge railway which used to bring phosphates from the mines along the Wadi Safaga at Umm el-Huweitat, and mountains "so tortured and bare that they look like skeletons of mountains" (de Monfreid).

453 kms: A fine mangrove swamp, with mangroves sitting on the water. Ahead are miles of white sand and pretty coves sparsely inhabited by Ababde fishermen. If you wish to swim or snorkel you should obey the usual rules: ask permission to camp, or leave the beach before sunset.

467 kms: Kidney Bay, marked by a plaque and with a camel police post.

480 kms: Another mangrove swamp.

482 kms: The village of Bir Quei, at the mouth of the Wadi Quei.

497 kms: A light railway bringing phosphates from the mountains crosses the road at el-Hamarawein, a company town with a large phosphate plant, company housing and schools, and a gas station. The port and jetty are at the southern end of the town.

510 kms: A lovely bay near the site of old Kosseir, the ancient settlement, is the setting for a tourist village designed by a student of Hassan Fathy, the internationally renowned Egyptian architect, and comprising chalets, restaurants, shops, a swimming pool, and a dive center. The village is due to open in 1989. Water will be piped here from Port Safaga. Minefields line the road on the outskirts of Kosseir.

516 kms: Kosseir.

Kosseir

History of the town From the earliest times Kosseir, called Taaou in pharaonic times, with an easy route to Koptos in the Nile Valley through the well-watered Wadi Hammamat, was an important port through which spices and perfumes from India, lapis lazuli from Afghanistan, copper from Oman, treasures from the land of Punt, and turquoise from Sinai traveled the trade route to Egypt, in exchange for wheat, granite, gold, ivory, and artifacts much sought after by other ancient states. The Ptolemies established Leukos Limen (White Harbor) a little to the south of old Kosseir, and used the new port, together with Myos Hormos and Berenice, to build up trade in the Red Sea. For some centuries Kolzoum (Suez) was the chief entrepôt in the Red Sea, but after its fall in the eleventh century this honor fell at times to el-Tor in Sinai, at times to Aidhab (now on the border with Sudan), and at times to Kosseir.

The route from the Nile to Kosseir was known to early European travelers, and was described by Thietmar, Bishop of Mersebourg, on a Christian pilgrimage in 1017. The Portuguese adventurer João de Castro came on an expedition in 1541 and had this to say: "Small and miserable, one of the worst places on the Red Sea, and the water is so salty you can't tell it from sea water. . . . Alcocer [Kosseir] is horrible to live in."

During the seventeenth century a rumor flourished that the Wadi Hammamat was in fact a distributary of the Nile which discharged into the sea at Kosseir. In the eighteenth century the route was sought after as a rapid way from Europe to India.

"At Cosseyr it rains frequently," complained the Comte de Forbin, passing through the town in 1817. He had come from Qena, where he observed

by the pacha's order, a road was then making to terminate at Jené [Qena]. The cachef [chief] of the district was employing whole tribes of Arabs in planting the caselier tree, intended to overshadow the road which is much frequented by the caravans of Cosseyr. It seemed strange, and not very consistent with our notions of the Arabs, to find them thus occupied, as scarcely any travellers, ancient or modern, have discovered and noticed in them an inclination for planting trees.

Obviously it was felt that the Kosseir route, by this time principally used by pilgrims embarking for Mecca, warranted such attention. Flaubert described the disaster of arriving at a well on the Kosseir road hot on the heels of another caravan, whose wading camels had so disturbed the water that it took a whole day to settle and become drinkable.

Baedeker's 1898 guide advised ten to eleven days for the journey from Qena to Kosseir and back (two to three more for Egyptologists) and suggested the caravanserai at Bir Ambar, three and a half hours from Qena, as a resting place for the first night. Built by Ibrahim Pasha for the Kosseir caravans and Mecca pilgrims, "It has no owner and is free to everyone to use as he likes. As nothing is done to keep it in repair, it is rapidly falling into decay."

Baedeker also described a feature of caravan routes called the *mabwala:* "Open places covered with camel dung. They occur on every great camel route at regular intervals and are of the utmost importance as sign posts showing the road. Hence no camel driver passes one of these places without giving his camels an opportunity to contribute their quota to the maintenance of the mabwala." Flaubert described several of these which he encountered during his journey through the Wadi Hammamat.

Edward de Montulé, who visited the region shortly after the Comte de Forbin, described Kosseir:

This town, which is the central point of communication between the Indies, Arabia, and Egypt, is important from its commerce, and although the houses are built of yellow bricks, they present an agreeable appearance. The harbour is small and shallow, but defended by breakers, against which the waves dash with great fury. The first object in Cosseir that engages the attention, is a citadel erected by the Caliphs, upon the parapets of which the Turks have erected battlements.

He was received by the treasurer to the cachef, and then taken to a khan, "a large dwelling where you hire unfurnished apartments, and are under the direction of a porter, who is not very particular as to the furniture he lends you; but having passed several nights in the Desert we thought it a palace." One knows how he felt. The cachef received them in his mansion beside the port, and they were regarded with some curiosity as being almost the first visitors in European dress. The cachef enquired whether they needed to purchase shells, and sent some

opposite, above: Sea turtle; below: Brown-spotted moray eel

fishermen out on their behalf with a boat, but "the moon being in her last quarter, the sea continued to rise, and we were only able to procure a small quantity of shells."

The local water was brackish, but the cachef had just built a cistern to store sweet water brought from Arabia: "It is extremely dear, and yet great quantities are consumed, on account of the influx of merchants and pilgrims from Mecca." From here, he made arrangements to travel to India on a trip which would be "very short and easy—a journey of thirty or forty days at most."

The town today

Kosseir today is much less horrible than it appeared to João de Castro, and is worth exploring for an hour or two. Bungalows and two-story town houses are painted white, saffron, or lavender, and the streets are kept remarkably clean by means of litter bins. A government rehousing project with rows of neat one-story terraced houses have mud-brick annexes to house domestic animals—one solution to the common complaint that new housing doesn't leave much room to spread out. A drive around the port area will reveal elegant administrative buildings and warehouses and old, sadly decaying dhows. The crumbling yellow ruins of Sultan Selim's sixteenth-century fortress are to be found near the central circle. The town contains a gas station, a bakery, and provision stores. Near the center is a very basic hotel, the Princess. Secluded places to camp can be found along the picturesque Wadi Ambagi, on the road to Qus in the Nile Valley.

In recent years the mining and export of phosphates have provided much of the sustenance for the community.

Kosseir to Berenice (258 kms)

Accommodation along this route:

Mersa Alam rest house (653 kms from Suez)
Dokki Shooting Club rest house (653 kms)

Dive sites along this route:

Mersa Alam (653 kms)

At **518 kms** from Suez: Junction of the streets leading to the port and the fortress, and south to Mersa Alam.

opposite: Blue clam

523 kms: Police checkpoint.

547 kms: A pretty inlet with mangroves and a small police post, where you may ask permission to camp.

551 kms: A muddy inlet at the mouth of a wadi.

559 kms: Another sheltered camping beach.

569 kms: Road to Umm Ghreg, with a few private houses on the beach.

South from here are stretches of coral reef to explore with a mask and a snorkel. Be sure to obey the usual beach rules: because of mines, keep to the tracks, and don't leave the road on the right-hand (inland) side.

578 kms: Mena Mersa Toronbi, a wide bay providing anchorage, with a camel police post. The inland side of the road is mined.

583 kms: A shallow, sandy bay with no police or Frontiers Administration (FA) camps to overlook it.

584 kms: Another small beach: this one has an FA post. Opposite is a dusty wadi through which an old paved road, broken and passable only to four-wheel-drive vehicles, reaches after a few kilometers a group of abandoned, crude, drystone dwellings, littered with traces of habitation and of the rose red lead ore worked by the departed miners. The lead mine, which opened and closed in the 1960s, is at the end of the broken road: here the ore seems to have been scraped off the side of the mountain, as well as burrowed out in galleries. The lumps of soft rock scattered about are in such vivid hues that they must be a paradise for artists who mix their own paints, in fact they seem to contain all the colors found in the Luxor tombs. Remember that lead ore is toxic. If you should touch it, wash it off your skin as soon as possible. The red dust seems to be everywhere. As my companion remarked, the lead must have been mined by red men.

Four or five kilometers in from the sea are several good camping spots, with shade provided by *saayil* (acacia) trees sheltering under the cliffs. The beach is good for swimming and snorkeling.

593 kms: Mersa Mubarak, a narrow bay.

593.5 kms: Mersa Umbarik, and the Umm Rus gold prospecting project.

600 kms: A wide, shallow, brilliant aquamarine bay.

602 kms: A pretty sandy cove at the mouth of a wadi, with a delta of bushes and reeds. The beach is sheltered for camping, which is possible as long as permission is sought from the nearby FA post.

605 kms: Red Sea Chemical Company sign to its talc mines.

610 kms: A small bay.

617 kms: A bay with a white sand beach at the end of a bushy wadi.

635 kms: Mersa Gebel Rasas, storage tanks overlooking a deep bay lined with white sand.

640 kms: A wide damp wadi and a pretty white sand bay near a military installation.

642 kms: Another bay and coral reef. Unfortunately banks along the roadside inhibit access. Some of the beaches along this stretch are fouled with oil.

644 kms: A small village in a reef-filled bay.

653 kms: Mersa Alam, and the junction with the road through Wadi Umm Khariga to Edfu, 230 kilometers away in the Nile Valley. Mersa Alam has a small harbor with a stone quay and a population of migrant workers employed in potash mining. In recent years the town has taken on more of an appearance of a settlement rather than a work camp, and many families and new housing schemes are in evidence. A rest house is situated back along the main road, opposite the jetty—accommodation can be arranged with Abdel Moneim who can be found through enquiring at the police station, next to the bus stop at the Edfu road junction. Almost on the corner of the junction is a gas station. The bakery is a charred-looking building near the mosque. The area around the town is heavily mined.

There are good offshore reefs in Mersa Alam, but no diving facilities. The Dokki Shooting Club arranges fishing expeditions and has a rest house here. Arrangements for accommodation must be made in Cairo.

A nature reserve has been proclaimed from Mersa Alam south to Gebel Elba, within the Sudanese area of administration. The hunting and shooting of wild birds and animals is strictly prohibited, not least to the Ababde and Bishareen tribesmen.

655 kms: FA post. One may only travel south of this point with a special permit issued by the army and endorsed by the Frontiers Administration Force, both of which have offices in Heliopolis. An ordinary tourist pass which entitles the holder to visit the area for diving or fishing may sometimes be obtained from the Police Intelligence office (*mukhabarat*) in Hurghada.

There are several pretty coves in which to swim and snorkel, unspoilt in this remote area. They are visited by few people apart from the military, who usually confine themselves to the famous air force base at Berenice supposedly used by the U.S. Rapid Deployment Force. Others free to come and go are the Ababde residents, and for them a public bus passes through. Keep to the tracks.

667 kms: The remains of the small harbor of Wadi Ghadir, with fishing boats drawn up on the beach.

668 kms: A bay rather too exposed to the road for camping, but good for swimming.

672 kms: Wadi Ghadir, a very wide shingly wadi studded with desert plants. Along here are very good camping sites. Many animal tracks show that the wadi is not as deserted as it seems.

701 kms: An Ababde village is tucked under the palms and *tarfas* (tamarisks) of the aptly named Wadi Gamal (Valley of Beauty).

732 kms: The phosphate mine of Abu Ghosun, a small company town of migrant workers with a large new mosque.

741 kms: A mangrove swamp set in a bay of unbelievable sapphire.

747 kms: An aquamarine bay with a shallow sheen of water over white sand. These remote beaches, sparsely inhabited by Ababde fishermen and visited by almost no one else, can still be spoiled by oil as ships empty their bilges with impunity.

752 kms: Mangroves running for several kilometers along the coast, ending with a broad flourish in a blue lagoon.

Mersa Wadi Ghadir

759 kms: Mersa Wadi Lahami, overshadowed by Gebel Hamata, a harbor with a small jetty and an FA camp.

776 kms: FA post (see below). On the left, a paved road leads to the tip of Ras Banas, passing a lagoon with a beach after 8 kilometers. Another 30 kilometers on is a deserted military installation. Three kilometers beyond this the road ends abruptly beside a Danger notice: the track goes to the left, skirting the fence of a minefield. The track continues over the barren peninsula of fossilized coral to the cliffs of Foul Bay. A little further along some old Arab dhows are drawn up on the beach in front of an Ababde village of simple huts built of ship boards, packing cases, and other flotsam.

Three kilometers beyond the village is the tip of Ras Banas, with an FA checkpoint and the tomb of Sheikh Banas, who came from Morocco in the nineteenth century: probably Sheikh Banas was a pilgrim who died at this point of the pilgrimage, though it is a mystery why he would have come so far south to cross to Mecca—unless, of course, he was shipwrecked. Nearby is an Ababde sheikh's tomb, a more simple affair with a circle lovingly built of coral flowers and shells, wooden poles decorated with flags of tattered fabric, and a precious piece of green satin wrapped round a stone at the head of the grave while masses of rags are tied to the stones round it. Gifts have been left by devotees: a book of matches, a shell, even a pretty Carmen tissue box. Other tombs of this type can be glimpsed over the hillocks all the way to Kosseir.

Retrace your route to the checkpoint at the main road.

It is extremely difficult to get past this point, and so on to the ruins of the Ptolemaic city of Berenice. You will need a special permit issued at the FA office in Cairo with "Berenice" clearly written on it, as distinct from "Ras Banas." For most travelers the journey along the Red Sea coast, if it didn't end at Mersa Alam, must end here; for those fortunate enough to be allowed further south the road will take you to the edge of Foul Bay (in Arabic Umm el-Ketef), "almost the whole stretch," according to the British Naval Intelligence Division in 1946, "foul with reefs and sunken rocks." Strabo, visiting Egypt around 25 B.C., described the bay, which he called Sinus Immundus (Foul Bay), in the last of the seventeen volumes of his geography.

Berenice was founded by Ptolemy II in 275 B.C., and named in honor of his mother. Its position as a junction of the trade routes from the Nile Valley, Africa, India, and the Near East made it a commercial center for the next five hundred years.

The ruins of the city and its temple are almost entirely covered by sand. In the distant hills are the famous but now exhausted ancient emerald mines of Wadi Sukeit and Gebel Zubara.

On the disputed border with Sudan to the south of Berenice is Gebel Elba, a lush area of tropical vegetation which the Ababde and Bishareen tribesmen share with mountain lion, ostrich, monkey, and gazelle. Protected by the laws of the Gebel Elba Nature Reserve, this phenomenal region is being studied by anthropologists and naturalists.

2
The Western Sinai Coast
(Suez to Ras Mohammed)

The Bible gave Sinai a bad name. "Would to God we had died by the hand of the Lord in the land of Egypt," the children of Israel complained to Moses, "for ye have brought us forth into this wilderness, to kill this whole assembly with hunger" (Exod. 16:3). For forty years they tried to find a way out of it, living as best they could. Food and fresh water were sparse and the terrain difficult. So it is not surprising that in the past there were few visitors to Sinai, and even today most travelers know its western coast road as the one you drive along as fast as possible, the sooner to reach St. Catherine's or Sharm el-Sheikh.

But take the time to pause, if you can. For, as Major C. S. Jarvis, a former governor of Sinai, said in his book, *Three Deserts:* "Sinai is like a Saville Row tailor, it does not display its goods in the shop window for all to see." From its western shore, renowned for its long sandy beaches where windsurfers can enjoy a day out of Cairo, roads lead off to the twelfth-century Qal'at el-Gundi (Soldier's Fortress), built to repel a Crusader invasion which never happened, and to the ancient turquoise mines of Serabit el-Khadim. There are beautiful wadis to explore, and the little town of el-Tor merits a visit.

45

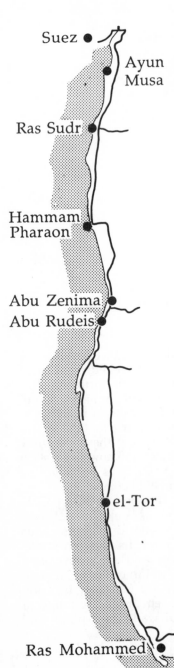

Suez
Ayun Musa
Ras Sudr
Hammam Pharaon
Abu Zenima
Abu Rudeis
el-Tor
Ras Mohammed

Earlier tourists would have taken their time. Baedeker's 1878 guide included this advice from "a veteran traveller among the Bedouin": "Take the railway from Cairo to Suez. Dispense with tents and beds; but take at least a couple of warm rugs to fold over the saddle, and to be used at night. Hire a boat at Suez, and procure an introduction to Shêkh Hennen at Tûr, and to the Monastery of Sinai. Pack preserved meats, and a few cooking utensils in a couple of baskets. No interpreter need be taken if the traveller speaks a little Arabic."

Alternatively, says Baedeker, camels under a Bedouin sheikh or a dragoman should be rented in Suez. "It is customary for the attendants to ask a backshish for every trifling service, but no attention should be paid to their demands. Another bad habit of theirs, to be carefully provided against, is that of tying up their beasts too close to the tents, and of chatting beside them half the night."

"The journey from Mt. Sinai to 'Akaba, and from Petra to the Holy Land," it goes on, "is very rarely undertaken, and should not be attempted without careful enquiry regarding the safety of the route." Nowadays one can, happily, travel quite safely on to Aqaba by means of the ferry at Nuweiba.

The modern-day traveler will find few places to stay between Suez and Ras Mohammed. Daghashland, 81 kilometers from Suez, provides a pleasant oasis, while the Tur Hotel in el-Tor is basic but clean, comfortable, and convenient.

The easiest way to reach South Sinai is through the Ahmed Hamdi Tunnel, 140 kilometers from Cairo.

Ahmed Hamdi Tunnel, Suez to el-Tor (261 kms)

Accommodation along this route:

Ras Sudr Holiday Village (60.5 kms)
Sudr Beach Hotel (60.5 kms)
Daghashland (81 kms)
el-Rabwa Club campsite (260 kms)

Diving facility along this route:

Daghashland (81 kms, arranges diving tours to Ras Mohammed)

Hoardings advertising services in Sinai mark the turnoff from the Suez road 119 kilometers from Cairo, 21 kilometers before the Ahmed Hamdi Tunnel, which was opened in 1980 and has greatly simplified communications with Sinai.

When passing through the tunnel it is forbidden to carry canisters of gasoline or butagas, and compulsory to carry a fire extinguisher. Each car pays LE 1 for a ticket, which is to be presented at the entrance. Observe the speed limit, and do not stop in the tunnel. Toilets are located behind the offices at either end. Three times a day convoys of ships can be seen passing through the canal almost over your head.

When making the return journey it is worth making the effort to reach the tunnel at least an hour and a half before sunset in order to reach Cairo by daylight. Although the road is now a dual carriageway (divided highway), driving standards of some truck drivers tend to be erratic.

Continuing from the tunnel, turn right at the crossroads towards el-Tor. The road straight ahead at the crossroads is signposted to Nuweiba. Don't worry if you miss this turn, as the roads will connect again later, though not until after the next gas station on the el-Tor road. (If you *are* making for Nuweiba cross-country, you'd better turn right anyway, as though to el-Tor, in order to fill up your tank.) You pass through a featureless, shingly stretch of desert, with occasional low hillocks.

At **5 kms** from the tunnel: Gas station, open 24 hours and selling soft drinks. On the right a short road leads to a military and commercial ferry. On the left is another junction with the road through the Mitla Pass to Nakhl and Nuweiba. You may either continue from Nakhl through Nakeb to reach the coast near Taba, or turn right before Nakeb (follow the signpost) along the road through the Wadi Watir to Nuweiba.

Along the Nakhl road, about one kilometer from the gas station, is a monument to 28,000 Yugoslav refugees who, with Allied help, fled Nazi occupation in 1944 and established a desert camp at el-Shatt (The Shore). They set up schools, a theater, and a newspaper, and stayed for two years, returning home at the end of the war. The memorial stands in the graveyard of the 526 refugees who died there, some as a result of their sufferings before being given refuge. The monument was renovated in 1985.

Suez sprawls on your right.

17 kms: Turn left for el-Tor. Ahead, the road carries on to el-Shatt at the mouth of the Suez Canal. Here the Israelis built a railway to bring supplies to the Bar-Lev line; now littered with tanks and railcars wrecked in the 1973 war, the trenches and sandbags of the Israeli fortifications present an unofficial military museum. On the opposite shore is Port Tewfik.

21 kms: For those traveling north, a signpost for the alternative road to the Ahmed Hamdi Tunnel.

24 kms: A sign beside a small cafeteria marks Strong Posts, the Ayun Musa military museum. Old Israeli fortifications are a paradise for Rambo-esque activities, while official graffiti give pause for thought.

26 kms: Ayun Musa (Springs of Moses): A large oasis watered by hot springs which cross under the gulf to erupt again at Ain

"Strong Point" military museum, Ayun Musa

Sokhna and Helwan, and believed to be the springs which Moses sweetened with a special tree. Once an important source of fresh water for shipping in the Gulf of Suez, it later became a residential suburb and, until the completion of the sweet-water canal in 1863, supplied water to Suez itself. Baedeker's 1898 guide described Ayun Musa thus:

> The property of M. Costa [the Russian vice-consul] and several Greeks, about five furlongs in circumference. The vegetation here is very luxuriant. Lofty date palms and wild palm saplings, tamarisks, and acacias thrive in abundance; and vegetables are successfully cultivated by the Arabs who live in the mud hovels near the springs. Their gardens are enclosed by opuntia hedges and palings. The springs vary in temperature from 70° to 82° Fahr.; some are only slightly brackish while others are exceedingly salt. The largest of them, enclosed by an old wall, is said to have been the bitter spring which Moses sweetened by casting a certain tree into it.

Ten minutes south of the gardens, marked by a solitary palm, Karl Baedeker saw a pool some four feet in diameter and one and a half feet deep of salt, bitter water measuring 70° F on a bed of black mud. On closer inspection he saw that the banks were composed of the carcasses of water beetles.

In the early part of the twentieth century Ayun Musa was a quarantine station for those returning pilgrims from Mecca not accommodated at el-Tor (see under el-Tor, below).

A sign on the right-hand side of the road, before you enter the oasis, leads along a well-trodden track to a well-oiled beach. Canal fees are levied according to weight, which unfortunately encourages ships to empty their tanks at the head of the Gulf, once so abundant with corals and shells. From the beach you can drive across the sand in a four-wheel-drive vehicle to the oasis: otherwise, go back to the main road and turn in on the right at the 237 kilometer sign to el-Tor (27 kilometers from the tunnel). The track leads behind the houses to a lovely spot—groves of palms, tamarisks, and mimosas (the gardens disappeared during the Israeli occupation when the wells were filled in). Near the "black" pool we came across the Russian embassy limousine resting in the shade while the ambassador and his wife bathed in the spring. The oasis was resonant with the song of small birds.

The reed-fringed pools at the southern end of the oasis are important for raptor migration—twenty-eight species of eagle, falcon, vulture, and buzzard, as well as storks, pelicans, and songbirds pause here en route from Western Russia and

Europe to Africa, taking advantage of thermal currents over the Gulf of Suez before turning inland at Hurghada.

28 kms: Police checkpoint. You will probably be waved on, though you may be asked to produce your passport or ID card, especially at checkpoints nearer to Sharm el-Sheikh. This is to check you are not traveling out of bounds on a pass issued in Taba. More rarely, traffic police will ask to check your car license.

Beyond Ayun Musa the shingly desert is sprinkled with war debris, minefields, and occasional scattered oases. Minefields are usually marked off with fences of tangled barbed wire and with oil drums with a pole standing through the center. To be safe, don't park your car or wander off the road along this stretch. On your right you can see the tip of the Gulf of Suez, the most northwesterly tongue of the Indian Ocean.

44 kms: High Way Rest House serving hot and cold drinks and meals of rice, kofta, and fried chicken. With a holiday village under construction, the rest house promises a row of small shops.

53 kms: Bedouin village at Wadi Laharta. The bushes are supported by a high water table just below the surface.

59 kms: Shell gas station, Happy Land campsite, and a right fork to Ras Sudr village. It is easier to find your way there, however, if you keep on the main road for another 2 kilometers.

60.5 kms: Ras Sudr junction, a hive of development with a new gas station, a mechanic and tire repair, a post office with a telephone, and a cafeteria. Turn right at the gas station for the holiday village of Ras Sudr and the Sudr Beach Hotel (the sign outside the hotel is written only in Arabic).

(B) Sudr Beach Hotel: The hotel is situated on a beach famous for windsurfing, but you must bring your own sailboard. You must also be prepared for the sad fact that the beach overlooks the vast silver tanks of one of Egypt's biggest oil refineries. At the entrance to the hotel is the impressive cartilage of a manta ray washed up after being hit by a propeller, and estimated to have weighed twelve tons. There are three types of accommodation: you can rent a rather dreary bungalow for five people, or a villa which sleeps up to sixteen, or you can stay in the hotel. The rooms have patios or balconies right on the beach. The hotel has two bakeries, one for French and one for local bread, and can provide bread for outsiders. There are two restaurants, one in the hotel and one about a mile along the beach—both are indifferent, and both are dry. There are no ashtrays in the hotel either, to discourage smoking. Reservations: (062) 70752. Cairo

reservations: Misr–Sinai Tourist Co., Misr Travel Tower, Abbasia Square, Telephone: 834356/821061. Fax: 830242. Telex: 93565 MSTCO UN.

64 kms: On the right, a road signposted Abu Suweira leads to a village and luxuriant plantations of wheat and fruit trees, fenced in by casuarinas and a variety of flowering trees.

A road leads left to Qal'at el-Gundi (Soldier's Fortress) 72 kilometers away, a twelfth-century fortress built by Salah el-Din to protect caravan and pilgrim routes and to augment his defenses in case of a Crusader invasion. Although ruined, the castle is an interesting detour if you have time to spare.

The road enters Wadi Wardan, a plain studded with "hedgehog" dunes formed by sand piling on and around rocks washed down from the mountains by flash floods. The growth on the dunes is sustained by minerals encased in the rocks. The old road runs along on the right.

The bushy area before Daghashland is a more private beach for camping and windsurfing than the next one, which is close to the road and often overcrowded. Show your passport at the police station on the corner before Daghashland; you have to drive past this on the way to the more private beach.

81 kms: Daghashland at the famous windsurfing bay of Ras Materma.

(B) Daghashland: A multicolored collection of canvas chalets each with two beds (an extra bed can be squeezed in), air conditioning, and a shower room. Owner Ali Daghash, who opened in August 1987, sees it as a pleasant summer resort for Cairenes, an alternative to the overcrowded Mediterranean coast. The public rooms are sunny and spacious, and there is a playground for children. The food could be a little more exciting. Tours to Ras Mohammed (252 kilometers away) can be arranged. Chalet rates vary for single, double, or triple occupancy, with special rates for children under twelve. Chalets can be rented by the day for LE 30 (four persons). Lunch (including entrance fee) is LE 18 per person. Reservations (necessary from June to September): 8 Ahmed Fouad Nessim, Nasr City, Cairo. Telephone: 609672/605884. Telex 93131 OIR UN

The beach at Ras Materma is safe for swimming and is popular in summer with day trippers from Cairo. If you bring your sailboard, don't stray far as windsurfers have been arrested after drifting away. Camping is allowed with permission from the nearest police post but there is very little privacy, so you may prefer to camp within the area of Daghashland for LE 5 per person per night, which includes the use of the hotel facilities.

98kms: Moon Beach village.

(B) Moon Beach: Opening 1990, with chalet accommodation, restaurants, disco, swimming pool, tennis courts. Cairo reservations: Nile Tower Building, 2 Taha Hussein Square, Zamalek. Telephone: 3400158/3412289. Fax: 3401658.

100 kms: Microwave tower on the left. Shortly afterwards a short track runs towards the sea. The beach, littered with ancient shells, leads to an uninteresting coral reef. Sandy swimming beaches, however, stretch for several kilometers south of this point. Remember that you must leave the beach before sunset unless you have permission to camp.

104 kms: Ras Malaab gypsum processing plant, followed by an old limestone quarry in the cliffs formed of recent fossilized limestone. The village of Gharandel is tucked back in the hills. The pyramid-shaped mountain of Hammam Pharaon looms ahead.

110 kms: Hammam Pharaon. A signpost and road to the right leads after 3 kilometers to a checkpoint, manned by a lonely policeman and his camel, beside a sign stating that entry to the Hammam Pharaon Health Spa is forbidden after 6:00 P.M. Beyond the beautiful, clear swimming beach in front of the checkpoint the air is soured by a strong smell of rotten eggs, and near-boiling water bubbles into the sea to nurture a bed of reeds. The springs have been used since time immemorial by Bedouin and travelers seeking a cure for rheumatism. Pharaoh's spirit is said to haunt the spot, and the 1878 Baedeker mentions that Pharaoh "boils eternally in the waters." His malevolent influence spreads to the sea, endangering passing ships. The springs themselves become hotter the higher up the mountain they go, but be careful because even at ground level you can burn your toes. A grotto leads to the caves that delve 50 meters into the rocks and are used as a natural sauna: the idea is that after sweating in the cave you plunge into the sea. The small road peters out, so you must return to the main road by the same route.

The main road, carefully engineered to guard against flash flooding, now turns away from the sea and enters a miniature limestone canyon. It is almost worth attempting to make this journey at different times of day in order to appreciate the changes in light and color.

117 kms: Turn sharp right. Take care when traveling in the northerly direction not to go straight ahead. This road goes to Wadi Gharandel, a green oasis.

121 kms: On the right, the small oasis of Bir Thal.

129 kms: Plantation.

131 kms: Bedouin village.

135 kms: Shortly before the date palm grove of Tayiba, a track, only suitable for four-wheel-drive vehicles, runs left through the Wadi Tayiba. The scenery is quite stunning, and perfect for camping underneath the limestone cliffs carved out by floods, although the ground is hard. If you still have the picnic lunch you brought from Cairo, though, this is the place to eat it. After 15 kilometers this track meets the road going to the abandoned ancient turquoise mines of Serabit el-Khadim (turn left: the mines are 50 kilometers away on a slow road). If you turn right here you will reach the coast again on a road which has been cut through the mountains and emerges 2 kilometers south of Abu Zenima (at 146 kilometers from Suez).

139 kms: (On the main road): The Tayiba oasis, through which, only a few decades ago, caravans passed taking coffee and spices from el-Tor to Suez for the European markets.

142 kms: The road meets the coast. Along the shore runs a narrow-gauge railway, which before World War II ran inland where it met the cableway from the mines at Umm Bogma.

146 kms: Abu Zenima. Karl Baedeker tells us that this spot, or more probably in the Wadi Tayiba, was the encampment of the Israelites on the Red Sea (Num. 33). The sprawling town today contains a gas station, post office, and provision store. It is worth noting that gasoline services in small towns like Abu Zenima depend on the electricity supply; if the power cuts off, so do the pumps. The inhabitants are mostly employed in the oil and mining industries.

Just south of the town are the remains of offices and warehouses of a British iron and manganese company, and of the pier from which ships would transport the ore to Suez, returning with drinking water, mail, and supplies.

South from here the road skirts the coast while mountains loom on the left, their different colors caused by sediments washing down from the heart of mineral-rich Sinai. The road rounds mountains which jut down to the coast and resemble mounds of scrunched-up paper.

Baedeker, traveling by camel, says the route skirts the sea for an hour and a half. "Travellers usually walk here, and amuse themselves by picking up shells, as Sinai travellers have done from time immemorial," at least, he continues, since "Thiedmarus in the 13th cent., . . . Fabri, and . . .

Breidenbach, the last of whom says, that 'various kinds of shells are to be found on the coast of the Red Sea, and also white coral, and many beautiful stones,' probably meaning by the last expression the smooth fragments of quartz on the beach."

155 kms: A police checkpoint situated just before a small oasis, with the remains of houses destroyed by floods. Here was the pharaonic port of Maghara (el-Markha) from where turquoise and copper were sent to fill the coffers of the Theban dynasties. The mountains open on to the wide plain of el-Markha—"not destitute of vegetation," according to Baedeker—and as the limestone ends the old, brown, rugged rocks begin. It is from these igneous rocks, grooved by sporadic rains, that Sinai's mineral wealth originates. From now on limestone will appear only as an occasional coastal fringe on the granite rocks.

165 kms: Abu Rudeis. On the left, a UN Peacekeeping Force outpost, and an airstrip connected with the military and the oil industry. On the right, a gas station, a post office with an international telephone, a clinic, a bakery, a supermarket, and a branch of the Bank Misr open for foreign exchange from 8:00 A.M. to 2:00 P.M., Sunday to Thursday.

167 kms: The road on the left goes through the Wadi Sidri to the turquoise mines of Wadi Maghara, and then swings round to the turquoise mines of Serabit el-Khadim and the Twelfth Dynasty temple of Hathor, the "Lady of Turquoise" and protective genius of Sinai, which also contains later inscriptions of Hatshepsut (Eighteenth Dynasty). The mine was worked more than 5,000 years ago for copper, malachite, and turquoise. The road circles back to Abu Zenima, and four-wheel-drive vehicles may take the track through the Wadi Tayiba previously described (see above at 135 kilometers).

187 kms: Oil storage tanks.

191 kms: Turn left for Sharm el-Sheikh and St. Catherine's. The private oil company road ahead goes to the oil fields of Abu Durba, where one of the 1979 Israeli handover ceremonies took place. There was never very much oil here, but whatever oil was to be found was exploited by the Israelis.

193 kms: War debris.

203 kms: The junction with one of the world's most beautiful roads, which wriggles through the picturesque Wadi Feiran to the Monastery of St. Catherine and on through spectacular mountain scenery to Sinai's eastern coast. The rest house on the corner offers hot and cold drinks, ice cream, snacks, and some unappetizing hamburgers. The toilets are fairly clean. There is no gas station: the next one is at el-Tor, 70 kilometers to the

opposite: Lionfish

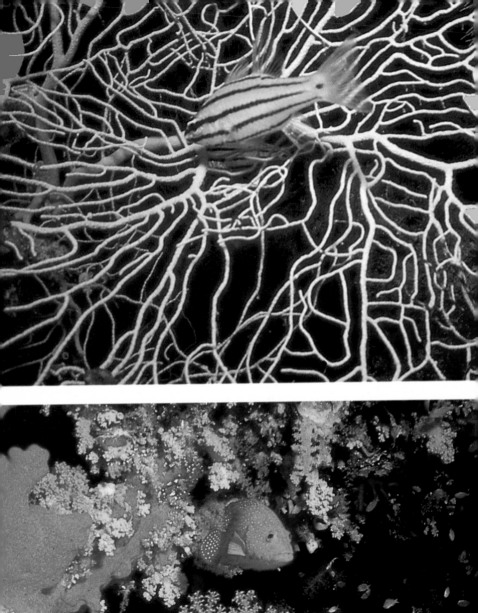

south. The checkpoint at the junction is operated by the traffic
police. The road enters the vast, bushy plain of el-Qa', which
looks as though it should once have been a sea- or riverbed but
bears no trace of shells. The Gebel Araba separates the plain
from the sea, while on the left looms the formidable range
which protects and dominates South Sinai, culminating in the
peaks of Gebel Musa (Mount Sinai, 2285 meters high) and
Gebel Katerina (2842 meters high).

The highest point on the left as you pass through el-Qa' is
Gebel Serbal (2089 meters high).

259 kms: Police checkpoint at a large oasis peopled by a mixture
of Bedouin and families from other parts of Egypt who have
sought employment in el-Tor. The road through the oasis was
washed away, together with several homes, during floods in
1986.

260 kms: A road on the right winds through this charming oasis
to Hammam Saidna Musa, the "Bath of Our Lord Moses," at
the foot of Gebel Musa. The warm sulphur springs have long
been used for general healing and for rheumatism, and have
been covered over and renovated under the patronage of
various rulers and pashas. They have now fallen under the
patronage of the South Sinai Travel Company, who opened
the el-Rabwa club, restaurant, and campsite in December 1987.
Use of the baths (which have a temperature of 37° C) is still a
modest 10 piasters; camping with use of the toilets is free is
you bring your own tent. The open-air restaurant sits a few feet
up the mountainside (don't drive up, or you'll have difficulty
in turning round) and commands a perfect view at sunset.

The plantations watered by the springs have belonged for
centuries to the monks of St. Catherine, whose right to the
land is protected by an edict of the prophet Mohammed. The
1878 Baedeker states, "One of the monks is stationed at Tûr,
officiating partly as a chaplain to a few Christians resident
there, and partly as a caterer for the monastery which is
supplied with provisions and fish from Tûr." Many hermits
and anchorites were drawn to Gebel Hammam Saidna Musa.

You can reach el-Tor by continuing past Hammam Saidna
Musa to the sea, and driving south along the beach to the
harbor.

At 261 kms from Suez: Back on the main road, the road forks
right to el-Tor, left to Sharm el-Sheikh. There is a gas station
on the by-pass.

opposite, above: Fan coral with camouflaged visitor;
   below: Spotted coral grouper

El-Tor

History of the town

Baedeker wrote of the town in 1878,

> Tûr is a place of some importance, inhabited by Arabs, whose property, estimated at several hundred francs, is partly derived from the numerous shipwrecks which take place near the island of Shadwan. The harbour is admirably protected by coral reefs, which, however, are dangerous to those unacquainted with their situation. Tûr affords the only good anchorage in the Gulf of Suez, besides Suez itself.

El-Tor was in a favored position: not only did it provide anchorage, but alone in almost all the northern Red Sea it possessed sweet water. It was not only a natural harbor but also a calling point for Suez-bound ships to collect water and fresh food, or to shelter when north winds made the passage to Suez impossible. Known as a port from the time of the Phoenicians, it was called Raithu by the Ptolemies. El-Tor's fortunes waxed and waned as it vied with Suez, Kosseir, and Aidhab for the goods from the entrepôts of Jeddah and Aden.

In 1058 el-Tor replaced Suez as the chief port in the gulf, and goods (and pilgrims) were transported overland to Cairo and Alexandria. Prominence later went to Kosseir, then to Aidhab, returning to el-Tor in 1378. Eventually, the customs center passed once again to Kosseir, and el-Tor, although it still provided food, water, and shelter, did not recapture its importance as a trade center. Its position was used to advantage, however, for it became the main quarantine station (run by the Egyptian Quarantine Board) for pilgrims returning from Mecca. Eyewitnesses of the great crush of 1929, when 29,358 pilgrims passed through, remember that the accommodation was good and arrangements very orderly. On the whole the health of the passengers was sound; more deaths occurred after emergency surgery in the hospital than from disease, and the only long holdup was in 1930 when a cholera carrier was discovered and all pilgrims were kept in el-Tor for eight days before being allowed on through the canal. The camp closed down in 1937, the few late arrivals that year being accommodated at Ayun Musa, and after that responsibility for the health of the pilgrims passed to the Saudi Arabian authorities.

The town today

El-Tor, a flat, sunsoaked town, is surrounded by "farms" or plantations producing vegetables and fruit. It is well worth exploring, with the areas of interest lying down by the sea. On the northern edge of the deserted harbor is the new, white-domed Japanese-built cultural center, and behind this the crumbled remains, no more than low brick walls on stone foundations, of a fortress built by the Mamluk Sultan Selim Murad I, who died in 1520. Excavating near the fortress, the Japanese have uncovered some Roman coins, in the process sweeping away several Bedouin squatter homes built of lumps of fossilized coral. The remaining houses stand by with their fisher families not knowing whether they are staying or going. Behind them is the church, an imposing yellow building, still affiliated to the Monastery of St. Catherine and protected by the same decree, although this did not save the "Forty Martyrs of el-Tor" from being massacred by Arab tribesmen.

One of the old trades of the town, happily abolished, was making sandals out of dugong skins.

Most of the signposts in el-Tor are in Arabic, so you will need to look for a few landmarks if you want to find your way around. The bus station and the Tur Hotel are opposite the hospital—to find them, head for the northern radio mast. A road on the right after the hospital runs to the harbor (half a kilometer). The South Sinai Governorate building is the large pink building trimmed with white, next to the Bank Misr, on the same side of the main road as the bus station, and the post office is along from here on the right. You can turn left past the post office to reach the Ras Mohammed road. The official buildings are isolated and spread out, as if waiting for things to happen around them.

A new dual carriageway (divided highway) runs along the coast towards the airport. The quarantine station is on this road just past the el-Wady Hotel: the four jetties, hospital, laboratories, warehouses, and boat mechanics' sheds are on the right, and the barracks spread over several acres on the opposite side of the road: many have been demolished, and others converted for housing. You can drive through the neat streets and easily imagine them teeming with returning pilgrims, all anxious to get home. The large stone houses around the quarantine buildings belonged to doctors and officials. The barracks are low, whitewashed buildings in a sad state of repair, the administration buildings have fallen roofs, and the stone houses have lost their windows. This piece of history must be attended to soon if it is to be prevented from falling into decay.

Beyond the airport is the village of Gibeil.

Near Ras Abu Suweira are "singing sands," once visited by curious tourists, now all but forgotten, where falling sand causes a strange noise.

Accommodation
There are two older local hotels, the *el-Wady* and one called simply *Hotel*, but they charge the same as, and are far inferior to, the *Tur Hotel* (C), which is approached from the concourse of the bus station and belongs to the East Delta Bus Company. It is clean and well furnished and has a TV lounge and a pleasant restaurant. All rooms have a bathroom and hot water. The set dinner is LE 5.00. Breakfast, LE 1.25, is not included in the room rate. Rooms have ultraviolet mosquito- eaters, and for an extra LE 1 you can hire a fan.

El-Tor to Ras Mohammed (87 kms)

At **266 kms** from Suez: The el-Tor by-pass, for those traveling north.
   The road now passes through a flood plain littered with boulders brought down from the mountains. In time, fertile sand enriched by the mineral deposits will pile up over the boulders, forming hedgehog dunes. On the shore is a wide belt of quicksand, used with expediency by turtles who can nest here undisturbed.
288 kms: War debris. Masked by heat haze, the mountains lie far back on the periphery of the sand flats.
301 kms: Microwave towers.
   The redness of the mountains is caused by a high concentration of iron oxide on the surface. From now on the mountains will dominate the coastline, and other changes will take place on the shore. The Gulf of Suez nowadays supports little coral, partly because of its low winter temperatures, but mostly because of the destruction of the reefs caused by oil and shipping. But the coral which begins here flourishes so well that within a few kilometers it forms perhaps the most spectacular diving site on earth.
333 kms: A solitary lighthouse marks the turnoff to Mahmaiet Ras Mohammed (Ras Mohammed Nature Reserve), clearly signposted on the right. The road is asphalted up to the police checkpoint.
After 15 kms: A pair of microwave towers near a shallow swimming beach with a long wade to deeper water.

After **16 kms:** Police checkpoint, where your car and passport numbers will be registered. A permit is not needed to enter, but no one is allowed to enter or leave the reserve after dark. The road becomes a dirt track for the next 4 kilometers to the cliffs of Ras Mohammed itself.

You will be reminded politely not to fish. Every effort is being made to implement the spirit of the reserve, but the authorities need the cooperation of the public. The rule is: don't take *anything* out of the sea. Divers should remember that the round trip from here to Na'ama Bay to refill their tanks is 50 kilometers via the new road to Sharm el-Sheikh.

Ras Mohammed

You will probably have two thoughts when you reach Ras Mohammed, and the second will be to wish all the other people away. If you want this wonderful place to yourself then avoid weekends altogether. There are no camping facilities, and as more and more tents spring up privacy has to go by the board.

The entire promontory is built of ancient coral, which rises out of the sea to over 60 meters and plunges to the same depth below. You can start your tour on the west side, where, just behind the

Shark Observatory, Ras Mohammed

Mangrove channel, Ras Mohammed

Black Hill, the right-hand fork leads to the Socony–Vacuum quay and the mangrove channel. Along the track just beyond the quay, on the left, in an enclosure marked by fossil coral rocks, is the Earthquake Position, a shallow rift filled with blue–green water. Straight ahead the track comes to the mangrove channel, a long inlet trimmed with bushy mangroves.

Back at the Black Hill, take the left fork to visit the rest of the reserve. The road forks again—the lower, right-hand track leads to Hidden Bay, a tranquil turquoise inlet. The higher and more rocky track leads to Ras Mohammed cliff (the Shark Observatory). The cliff is accessible, but the terrain is very difficult, even with four-wheel drive. You will have to take it slowly and make several recces to avoid disaster.

The lagoon near the mangrove channel is an ideal spot to practice windsurfing.

Dive sites

Socony–Vacuum Quay: The quay can be found by keeping to the right-hand track behind the Black Hill after going through the police checkpoint. Enter through the sandy lagoon to the left of the quay, where the reef table is less than 3 meters wide, and drops almost vertically to 40 meters. Turn right, and continue along the reef edge. A second dive may be made on the left of the quay.

Shark Observatory: This is the richest area for marine life in the Red Sea, and undoubtedly one of the best dive sites you will ever visit. Here are the big fish: sharks, napoleons, and schools of jack fish and tuna, as well as countless species of smaller creatures teeming round the reef. Do, therefore, plan your dive carefully and don't get carried away with exhilaration, and remember that the reef wall drops to just over 80 meters. The huge cliff faces southeast: enter from the point just on the right of the rock. You may turn left or right. A second entrance is from the square-shaped camping beach around the next point to the south, but the reef table here is very wide and entry is only possible at high tide, when the water is calm. Again, turn left or right.

Eel Garden: A third entrance, and one more suitable for less-experienced divers, is on the north side of the Shark Observatory rock. Here is an easy entry across a sandy beach and a narrow reef table, which brings you to the biggest eel garden in the area. Dive to the right or the left, again two dives from one spot.

Shark Reef: It is not recommended to swim out to the two reef patches directly south of the Shark Observatory; these should be enjoyed from a boat dive.

The Alternatives: A group of small islands to the west of Ras Mohammed, so named because although not the best dives, they provide an alternative dive site for those who would like a change from the regular dive sites.

Mersa Bareika and *Ras Atar:* Boat dives. Interesting sites at present inaccessible due to strict military control of the coast.

3

The Eastern Sinai Coast
(Ras Mohammed to Taba)

While the debate rages as to whether Australia's Great Barrier Reef or the Gulf of Aqaba is the world's greatest dive site, all divers agree that the Gulf of Aqaba comes out on top in one respect—accessibility. Though Sinai conjures up pictures of mystery and remoteness, it is in fact easy to reach, being linked directly by air to Europe and no more than a few hours' drive from Cairo. Above all most of the corals are in fringing reefs, reached by stepping off the beach and putting your mask under the water—no need for expensive boat trips. Camping can bring the cost of your diving holiday right down. Yet even on this well-known shore are unspoilt, virgin reefs teeming with beautiful fish and marine life, and numerous wrecks driven on to the treacherous reefs of the notorious Straits of Tiran provide additional spectacular interest.

Once you have passed Ras Mohammed you will encounter little danger from sharks—reef sharks in the Gulf of Aqaba are well fed and not interested in eating you. Turtles and manta rays abound, and the reef fishes from tiny golden anthias (goldfish) to parrot fish to giant wrasse present vivid and unforgettable colors.

Na'ama Bay, Dahab, and
Nuweiba are established tourist
centers and it is no longer necessary,
as it used to be, to pack every piece of
camping equipment you needed down
to the last drop of washing water.
Camping gas cylinders can be bought
in Na'ama Bay, fish and chips in
Nuweiba, and chocolate pancakes in
Dahab. The planned opening of
Nuweiba airport and the shorter
road through Nakhl will bring the
central east coast closer to Cairo and
to Europe. The road to Taba cuts along
the shore; you don't have to force
your jeep or your camels around the
headland through the waves as you
did until a few decades ago. The
Egyptian government is planning to
build a bridge to link Sinai with
Saudi Arabia near the Straits of
Tiran. The bridge, eight kilometers
long, would be constructed to allow
the passage of ships through to the
ports of the Gulf of Aqaba.

Eastern Sinai, in short, is easier to
get to and to travel around in than it
used to be, but its stunning scenery
does not change, and whether you
will tear yourself away as easily as
you arrived is another matter.

Ras Mohammed to Sharm el-Sheikh (27 kms)

At **333 kms** from Suez: Turnoff to Ras
Mohammed.

342 kms: Ras Mohammed can be
glimpsed through a gap in the
crags. As you are passing through
a military area and the rocks on
either side are honeycombed with
fortifications it is absolutely
forbidden to leave the road. This

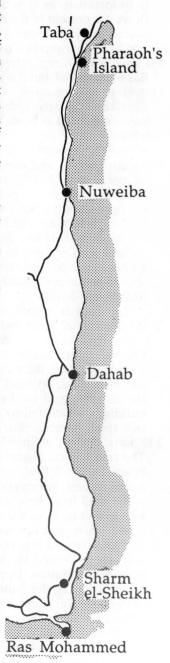

is unfortunate as it is a geologist's paradise: traces of lava flows are present in the richly colored volcanic rocks, part of a sedimentary plateau. A river terrace is visible to the right and left, superimposed on the solid geology.

354 kms: Army camp. A track formerly led round the shoreline to Ras Mohammed, but it is now out of bounds, and it is not known if it is still passable. Offshore is the dive site of Mersa Bareika, similarly forbidden, and recently warning shots have been fired at boats attempting to anchor.

356 kms: First of the four checkpoints at the entrance to Sharm el-Sheikh, this one manned by Egyptian traffic police.

357 kms: Second and third checkpoints, manned by Egyptian border guards. Foreigners, and sometimes Egyptians, will be asked to produce passports or identity cards. People coming in the opposite direction and holding Sinai tourist passes issued in Taba, which are valid for fourteen days and allow access to the eastern Sinai and St. Catherine's, cannot go beyond this point. Those wishing to extend this period (bear in mind that a fine is imposed for overstaying) or to travel to Suez or Cairo should obtain a normal tourist visa from the passport office in Sharm el-Sheikh.

The fourth checkpoint is controlled by the MFO (Multinational Force and Observers).

The road rounds a corner, and before you is Sharm el-Sheikh, unfortunately often abbreviated to "Sharm" which is a bit like calling the place "Bay" (or "Cove"). The new and, it has to be said, artificial little town sits on top of the cliff on the other side of the bay. At its foot lies a hodge-podge of buildings which follow no pattern at all at first glance, and two small harbors, Sharm el-Sheikh and Sharm el-Moiya.

360 kms: Sharm el-Sheikh harbor, a civil and military port. The next harbor, Sharm el-Moiya, contains a marina for small boats. On the left of the road is the Yacht Club, with simple rooms for rent, members only.

The road forks here, one branch leading to the town on the hilltop and to Taba, the other to a low row of shops with blue doors where you can find several cafeterias selling tasty fish and local food, a supermarket of sorts, a bazaar, and a garage workshop. Behind the shops is a bakery, and round to the right a gas station. Opposite the gas station, in a detached white villa, is the Sandy Palace Restaurant, which serves oriental food at about LE 8 per head.

Occasionally a ferry leaves from the harbor on a six-hour trip to Hurghada. A one-way ticket is LE 45 from South Sinai Travel, Ghazala Hotel, Na'ama Bay.

For Na'ama Bay and Dahab, turn left at the foot of the hill.

Sharm el-Sheikh

The Israelis chose this hilltop, with its Hollywood mountain backdrop, commanding a view from Ras Mohammed to the Straits of Tiran, to build a small town. Apartment blocks dominate the approach; below them is the city council, the bus station, and the tourist police station. At the top are two banks (the Bank of Alexandria and the National Bank of Egypt, open from Mondays to Saturdays from 7:30 A.M. to 2:00 P.M., and on Sundays from 10:00 A.M. to noon), a post office with a long-distance telephone, a branch of South Sinai Travel, a greengrocer, two supermarkets, and several restaurants. A new hotel is being constructed in a style similar to that of the apartments. To the east of the square, a road runs past the Youth Hostel to Clifftop Hotel.

Accommodation

Note: To reach the Sharm el-Sheikh operator for connections to local extensions, dial 10 or (062) 770895/771931.

The Sharm Hotel (located on the small bay below Sharm el-Sheikh) and the Hilton Holiday Apartments (on top of the cliff) are due to open in 1990. In addition, private houses are being constructed past the Hilton Apartments on the cliff edge. Many of these will be rented on long or short term leases: contact individual owners for availability.

(B) Clifftop: This Israeli-built hotel sits, as its name suggests, beside the elevated town of Sharm el-Sheikh. To reach it turn left at the top of the hill leading to the town and continue behind the Youth Hostel. The hotel has much improved in recent years and is popular with those who don't want to "live it up" in Na'ama Bay and prefer its relaxing atmosphere, friendly staff, and good food. In fact it makes a special effort because it is not in the bay, and relies a lot on recommendation. Guests stay in bungalows surrounded by pretty gardens. Tents are also available (price range C). The set lunch or dinner is LE 12. Diving video films are shown, and excursions can be arranged by taxi or jeep to Ras Mohammed or to the mountains, but diving equipment has to be hired from one of the diving clubs in Na'ama Bay. There is a regular taxi service from here to the airport, the harbor, and Na'ama Bay. Reservations: Sharm el-Sheikh: (062) 770448 or operator ext. 541. Cairo: Sinai Hotels and Diving Clubs, 32 Sabry Abu Alam, P.O.ʳ Box 2336 (located just off Suleiman Pasha

Square). Telephone: 3930200/3930301/3931543. Telex: 94002 OHTEG UN.

(B) *El-Kheima*: Hotel and dive center, with air-conditioned rooms, huts, tents, restaurant, and bar. Located down the hill near the Yacht Club. Cairo reservations: 78 Sawra Street, Heliopolis. Telephone: 2907866/2903513. Fax: 3417998. Telex: 20581 PRO UN

(C) *Youth Hostel*: Turn left at the top of the hill when you reach the town. The hostel is for Youth Hostel members only; accommodation is in dormitories for LE 3 per person per night. The hostel opens from 6:30 to 9:30 A.M. and from 2:00 to 10:00 P.M. in winter, 2:00 to 11:00 P.M. in summer.

Dive sites

NOTE: Diving equipment must be hired from one of the dive clubs in Na'ama Bay, 7 kilometers down the road.

The Temple: From the square, continue south past several lots on which private villas are being constructed. Out to sea on your right is this dive site famous for boat night dives.

Ras Umm Sidd: Although the track looks rough, you don't need four-wheel drive to visit this dive site. The promontory of Ras Umm Sidd is approached from the lighthouse: to reach it, turn left at the end of the tarmac road (which circles back to Sharm el-Sheikh) at a point marked by an oil drum, and follow the well-beaten track. Pass through the police checkpoint at the lighthouse—the guard will let you through when he sees your gear. If you wish to camp along here this is where you should ask permission, although the rocky ground does not provide the best campsite along this coast. After the checkpoint the track winds down to the cliff top, from where there are steps erected in 1987 by Cairo Divers leading to the entrance. Snorkel over the shallow reef. This is a beautiful dive, but there is a strong ebb current so keep close to the reef or you may be taken out to sea. As in all the sites round the Sharm el-Sheikh area where they are used to wetsuited intruders, the fish welcome you in search of tidbits. As you feed them they will swim up to your mask and slip through your fingers to snatch the food, but once it is gone they lose interest and keep their distance. Although feeding the fish can be an occasional treat both for them and for you, it is not a good idea to feed them too much or too often, as they may come to rely on what is a poor substitute for a natural diet.

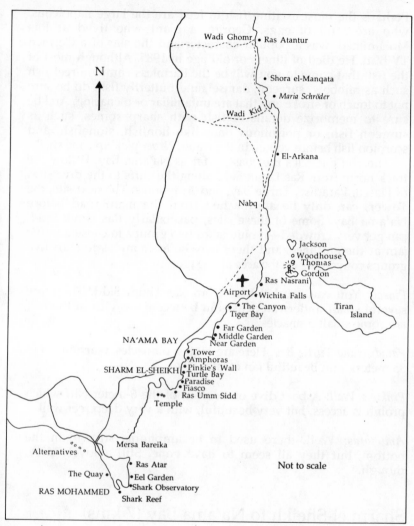

Sharm el-Sheikh dive sites

Perhaps the most exciting fish to feed are the large napoleons, who are fond of eggs. George, a giant who lived at Ras Mohammed, was a popular character and the star of a German TV film. He died of illness or old age in 1985. Although most of the fish that come to you will be the harmless common reef fish such as rainbow, surgeon, damsel, and butterfly fish, do be sure not to touch or stroke any that are unfamiliar or menacing. And be sure to memorize details of fish with sharp spines, such as surgeon fish, or poisonous ones like lionfish, stonefish, and scorpion fish before you go in the water. *Never* pick up cone shells.

The reef encircles the coast as far as Na'ama Bay. Follow the track north from Ras Umm Sidd along the cliffs to the dive sites of Fiasco, Paradise, Turtle Bay, and Amphoras. The next site, the Tower, can only be approached from the main road before Na'ama Bay. Some of these sites, particularly Ras Umm Sidd, can get very crowded—it only takes two groups to cause a traffic jam at the entrance, and there may be as many as four or five groups converging on the area at one time.

Fiasco: You can snorkel here from Ras Umm Sidd. There are several small underwater caves in between; away from the reef are some small pinnacles.

Paradise and Turtle Bay: Here are higher pinnacles, reaching 25 to 35 meters, and beautiful fan corals.

Pinkie's Wall: A boat dive on account of the 6-meter cliff which prohibits access, but very beautiful, with a very deep reef wall.

Amphoras: Well, there used to be amphoras strewn on the bottom, but they all seem to have gone. Still a lovely dive, though.

Sharm el-Sheikh to Na'ama Bay (7 kms)

At **361 kms** from Suez: At the foot of the Sharm el-Sheikh hill, turn north at the sign to Taba. A bus is scheduled to run from Sharm el-Sheikh to Na'ama Bay and on to the airport at Ras Nasrani every half hour or so throughout the day, although the wait is usually longer. The bus stop is at the foot of the hill, on the Taba road. The last bus runs at about 11:00 P.M.

363 kms: Pull over and look back towards Sharm el-Sheikh. Your eye will fall on a prominent rock which from this point dramatically resembles the head of the late John F. Kennedy.

364 kms: Sharm el-Sheikh by-pass on the left.

365 kms: The Tower. Away on the right-hand side you will see a plantation known as Sharm Farm, behind which lies the dive site of the Tower. The track to the farm leaves the main road at the point where a fallen pylon lies near the road. Turn left before you reach the farm, passing a wrecked bus which should be on your right. The track veers left again and then falls steeply towards the sea, turning south. Now the track forks: take the left-hand fork to the Patio, a pleasant spot for camping. The right fork leads to a small, sandy beach set in a pretty cove. The Tower—a tall rock—rises on the far side of the little bay. This continuation of the reef from Ras Umm Sidd is thoroughly enjoyable both for divers and snorkelers, and the beach is fine for picnics, though less desirable for camping as one of the tour companies has established a permanent tent here. In spite of the sandy beach the cove is also unsuitable for swimming, as the coral comes up to the water's edge.

A word of caution: when ships in difficulty in the Straits of Tiran have opened their bilges, oil slicks have drifted over to this line of coast to settle on the reef. Check that the sand is clean, as oil has a habit of lurking almost unseen.

366 kms: The road on the right leads to the main MFO camp and is restricted to authorized traffic.

368 kms: Na'ama Bay. A road signposted The Beach runs down to the south side of the bay, ending at the jetty just beyond the Marina Sharm Hotel.

Na'ama Bay

Na'ama Bay is the heart of diving and social life in Sinai; with its white dive boats bobbing on the water, and the colorful flower gardens of the Marina Sharm Hotel, it can best be seen in the spring when the sunshine falling on the white-domed hotels is less blinding. The bay runs from the Marina Sharm Hotel and the Red Sea Dive Club in the south, and swings on a broad brick walkway past the Aquanaut Club, the Ghazala Hotel, the Fayrouz Hilton, and the Aquamarine, and on to the Gafy Camp. Lying back across a broad empty strip, where camels wander on the lookout for scraps, are the Camel Dive Club, the Sanafir Hotel, and the Shamandoura Snack Bar and Supermarket.

Theoretically you can stay, according to your means, anywhere from the Hilton to one of the campsites—that is if you can find space at the hotel of your choice. You can eat gourmet food in a restaurant or fry up on your camping-gas stove, and you can choose equipment from one of six dive centers. This is one of Egypt's fastest-growing resorts, and now that tents have been swept off the beach and much of the ramshackle scruffiness has gone you can stroll from one end to the other along the fairly evenly matched brick path, breathe in the sea and the mountain air, and imagine you are a million miles away from the turmoils of the Middle East.

The priority for 80 percent of visitors to Na'ama Bay is scuba-diving. Air and equipment are available at any of the dive centers on presentation of a valid diver's card; if you do not have one you must take a course of instruction. Most divers do not carry their own tanks or weight belts, and these are easily obtainable—in fact all necessary articles can be hired, including, of course, snorkeling gear. You can arrange half- or full-day dive trips with the clubs by jeep or boat when you arrive, or you can book in advance (see details at the end of this section). Trips can also be taken into the mountains with a Bedouin guide by jeep or camel, or both; arrangements can be made with South Sinai Travel, Sanafir Hotel, or the Camel Dive Club. Most of the hotels run excursions by arrangement.

Many tours leave at about eight in the morning so check beforehand that an early breakfast is available at your hotel or campsite, for while it is inadvisable to snorkel or dive on a full stomach it isn't a good idea to take on fairly heavy physical exercise when you are starving either. Dehydration sets in very quickly in air as dry as this so always take bottled water with you on expeditions and remember to drink water, tea, or soft drinks whether or not you are on the move. If you want to spend the day sunbathing remember that from April to October, and longer if your skin is very fair, a maximum-protection sunscreen is recommended. When snorkeling in the summer, wear a T-shirt.

The weather in South Sinai is equable all the year round, and the winds on the southern tip of the peninsula are rather less obtrusive than they can be in Dahab or Nuweiba. Nevertheless cold spells are experienced and warm clothing is necessary in the evenings of the winter months. Snorkelers usually find they need to wear wetsuits from November to March, depending on the weather which of course varies slightly from year to year. If you arrive and find it too cold to swim you can hire a wetsuit for about LE 20 a day.

Scuba divers should take the usual safety precautions, and should seek advice on the various dives from the friendly and helpful staff at the diving clubs. The underwater experience can be so enthralling that you can get carried away at times, so be sure to check and recheck your dive tables. Unfortunately there is

opposite: Goldfish linger round a coral head

no decompression unit in Na'ama Bay, and no sign yet of the planned fully equipped hospital. Accident victims used to be flown by the American unit of the MFO to Eilat, but they are understandably reluctant to do this as they are forced to break a string of military regulations. Officially victims are flown to Cairo, but they must wait for a scheduled flight and then transfer some distance from the Cairo airport to the hospital near Heliopolis. It need hardly be said that divers should avoid getting into trouble at all costs; happily, very few accidents do occur. For stings or minor injuries report to the dive center: if necessary you will be referred to the hospital at Sharm el-Sheikh or at el-Tor.

Interrupted only by the MFO camp and by Na'ama Bay itself, the coral reef swings round to Ras Nasrani. Excursions to all the sites are arranged by the dive clubs according to demand and include transport, weights, tanks, and a guide. All the sites can be reached by boat, and of course you must arrange with one of the clubs if you want to visit the island dives or any of the wrecks.

If you wish to visit the coastal sites yourself your dive will be determined by your vehicle. Four-wheel-drive vehicles are essential for trips to Middleland Far Gardens, Wichita Falls, and the Canyon (not to be confused with the Canyon at Dahab), and useful for Ras Mohammed. Ordinary cars, however, will easily be able to reach Nabq by following the road north of Ras Nasrani. Tracks also lead to the coast from points on the main road, but they are poorly marked and difficult to find for the first time, and are only for vehicles with four-wheel drive.

Evening entertainment and bars are run by the hotels. Afraid guests might be bored après-scuba, the Hilton arranges quite an elaborate social life. Other visitors prefer to stroll beside the beach or gather in the snack bar next to the Shamandoura Supermarket, which now and again gets its hands on a good cassette tape. The supermarket opens from 9:30 A.M. to 3:30 P.M., and from 5:00 P.M. (winter) or 6:00 P.M. (summer) to 10:30 P.M. (winter) or 11:30 P.M. (summer), and sells emergency supplies of food, toiletries, and beach articles. It also sells post cards which will be posted for you as long as you can provide the stamps and your friends can bear the wait—letters and cards take several weeks to arrive in Europe or the United States. The nearest post office, whose service is no quicker, is in Sharm el-Sheikh.

Travel agents

You can negotiate a hiking and camel-trekking tour to the mountains yourself. The going daily rate for a camel is LE 25, but you will need to pay for a pack camel and one for your guide. When a Bedouin agrees on a price he sticks to it: he will not

opposite: Clownfish in sea anemone

expect backsheesh, and his timekeeping will be exemplary, but equally he will expect you to keep your side of the bargain. However you will probably find it easier to ask at your hotel or dive center if you are interested in what for most people is an unforgettable experience. Some travel agencies specialize in these tours.

South Sinai Travel: SST has a wealth of experience in the area. Presumably because they spend so much time in the mountains, partners and employees can be distinguished by their beards which they wear as a hallmark. The head office is located in the Ghazala Hotel, where it complements the services of Sinai Divers. Sample excursion fares include a half-day trip to St. Catherine's for U.S. $22, a full-day camel safari U.S. $28, a two-day safari with all meals U.S. $70, and a Bedouin dinner and campfire U.S. $25. SST is the agent for the ferry which leaves occasionally for Hurghada (see Sharm el-Sheikh harbor). They also have a few bikes to rent.

In Cairo, *Oonas Tours* (telephone 668747/674153) runs diving trips to Na'ama Bay, while *Gezira Travel* (3410585/3410312) can arrange weekend packages which include bus travel and two nights in the Fayrouz Hilton.

Dive centers
All the centers in Na'ama Bay stress that divers need personal service and a sense of security, and that they can best be accommodated in small groups, in a small center with a warm atmosphere, not in an environment where they might become nervous and anxious. All the centers offer introductory dives, beginners' courses, night dives, excursions for divers and nondivers, and rental of all gear. Before you hire equipment decide whether you will get full use from it: the price is the same whether you hire for an hour or a day. Rates are much the same and most centers offer discounts in certain circumstances, for example to marine biologists or to members of Cairo Divers. In most cases the centers cooperate with one another to cope with demand. Do reconfirm course bookings and boat charters. As a rule centers do not take credit cards. Divers not under instruction must be in possession of a valid diver's card.

Red Sea (near the jetty and Marina Sharm Hotel), *Aquanaut* (on the beach in front of Shamandoura Supermarket), and *Aquamarine* (next to Hilton Fayrouz Village): These three centers are linked and are run under the general direction of the Sinai Company for Hotels and Diving Clubs. Between them they operate two boats—the *Tom* and the *Apuhara*—which take parties of up to twenty divers out for up to three days, meeting individual requirements (even vegetarian food!). They also run shore dives in four-wheel-drive vehicles, trips by minibus to sites around Dahab, and can arrange camel trips (for example to Ras Abu Galuum, north of Dahab, see below). A full-day diving package including two dives, transportation, guide, tank, weight belt, and unlimited air is U.S. $35 (Egyptian pounds are accepted). A full day to Ras Mohammed is U.S. $45, an introductory dive U.S. $40, and a private dive with a private guide U.S. $25. A five-day package deal including ten dives and one boat trip is U.S. $165, and a ten-day package deal costs U.S. $300. A five-day course leading to a certificate can also be arranged.

Snorkel trips include a half-day jeep trip, minimum four persons, for U.S. $40. Places may also be available for snorkelers on boat trips. If you prefer not to get wet you can have a 40-minute boat trip in a glass-bottomed boat for LE 4.

Rental of equipment includes a full wetsuit for U.S. $6.50, a 15-liter tank for U.S. $5.00, and a weight belt for U.S. $2.00. Air refills range from U.S. $2.50 for a 10-liter tank to U.S. $4.00 for a 20-liter tank. Rates for rental and excursions are lower for Egyptian nationals.

Cairo office: Sinai Hotels and Diving Clubs, 32 Sabry Abu Alam, P.O. Box 2336. Telephone: 3930200/3930301/3931543. Telex: 94002 OHTEG UN. Or contact through Marina Sharm Hotel.

Sinai Divers: Two popular old hands at Na'ama Bay, Rolf Schmidt and Petra Röglin, can be found at Sinai Divers' spanking new office in the Ghazala Hotel. Sinai Divers offers PADI, NAUI, and CMAS diving courses, full rental services, and trips lasting up to ten days on the boats *Ghazala I* and *II*.

Prices are U.S. $35 for a full day with two dives, U.S. $40 for a day trip to Ras Mohammed, U.S. $40 for an introductory dive, U.S. $20 for a night dive, and U.S. $175 (including equipment) for a five-day open-water course. Windsurfing is also on offer at U.S. $5 an hour. Rental includes U.S. $1.50 for a mask, U.S. $2 for boots, U.S. $4 for a 12-liter tank, and U.S. $3 for a refill. Major credit cards are accepted.

Sinai Divers: Sharm el-Sheikh, Block 1, Office 9. Telephone: (062) 771348/770217; direct Cairo line 771248. Fax: (062)771349. Telex: 66037 GAZAL UN. Cairo office: 79 el-Merghany Street, 11th floor, Heliopolis. Telephone: 672441/664013/664512/672064. Telex: 21364 SSTHQ UN/22996 SST UN.

Camel Dive Club: Hisham Gabr Aly, an anthropologist, runs the Camel Dive Club. Hisham offers a range of tours and courses that include a full-day diving package in Sharm el-Sheikh or Nabq for U.S. $35, a day at Ras Mohammed for U.S. $40, a five-day package deal for U.S. $165, and a five- to six-day diving course for U.S. $200 (LE 270 for Egyptian nationals). The club's boat, *King Senefer II*, is available for day and weekend charters. It can be chartered for a weekend for seven divers including tanks, weights, and a diving guide for U.S. $650. Food is not supplied, and you must bring your own sleeping bag. The galley is equipped with a refrigerator and a stove. A day charter costs U.S. $350 for up to ten divers. Hisham can also arrange camel safaris into the mountains, to visit the Bedouin farms and water holes, accompanied by Bedouin guides and lasting up to seven days. Free camping is available to clients at the back of the club, with the use of the shower. Bookings: (062) 771551 or Sharm el-Sheikh operator ext. 524. Fax: (062) 771552. Telex: 66036 HISHK UN.

D.T.M.: From an office adjoining the Fayrouz Hilton Village D.T.M. offers boat and shore dive excursions. Trips are prearranged: if you want to go along, add your name to the list on the notice board. A half-day excursion by boat or jeep costs U.S. $20, or U.S. $40 with complete equipment hire. A full-day snorkel excursion is U.S. $10. A full-day excursion to Ras Mohammed is U.S. $45. Ten-dive packages and beginners' courses are also available. Full rental of equipment at similar prices to the other centers.

Bookings can be arranged in Germany through D.T.M., Altheimer Eck 13, 8000 München 2. Telephone: 089 260 9421. Or through the Fayrouz Hilton.

Accommodation
The Tiran Hotel (next to Camel Dive Center), the Kanabesh Hotel (next to Aquanaut Dive Center), and the Victoria Hotel are at various stages of completion.

(A) Fayrouz Hilton Village: Opened near the end of 1987. It takes a while to get used to the arrangement of the Fayrouz Village. Instead of a lobby, guests check into a sort of cupboard. With no communal rooms apart from the restaurant and the bar this must make it very bleak in the winter. But the bar, originally designed as a discotheque, is very large; there is a pleasant terrace, a swimming pool, and stone-built bungalows equipped with most things sun soakers need including a hair dryer. Every evening except Sunday guests are serenaded by live music, and most evenings entertainment is arranged, from a Bedouin dinner

complete with camels at sunset to a paella evening or a barbecue. The table-d'hôte dinner is LE 22 inclusive. Diving services are provided by D.T.M., and highly-priced water sports include sailing, water-skiing, and windsurfing. Major credit cards accepted. Reservations: (062) 770504/770501; direct Cairo lines: 760575/769400. Fax: (Cairo) 770726. Telex: 66036 HISHK UN. Cairo reservations: Central Reservations Office, Ramses Hilton. Telephone 754999/758000.

(B) Ghazala: Opened in October 1987, the Ghazala's ghastly "bungalows" belie their pleasant if inappropriate Canadian pine-style interiors. Facilities include a swimming pool, tennis and squash courts, a discotheque, and the services of South Sinai Travel and the Sinai Divers Club. The buffet dinner is LE 18 plus taxes. Major credit cards accepted. Reservations: (062) 770217; direct Cairo line: 771284. Telex: 66037 GAZAL UN. Cairo reservations: Ghazala Hotel, 10th floor, 79 Merghany Street, Heliopolis. Telephone: 672441, 672964, or 664013. Telex: 21364 or 22996.

(B) Marina Sharm: Like the Clifftop, the Marina was built by the Israelis and is now managed by the Egyptian government-run Sinai Company for Hotels and Diving Clubs. It occupies the southern reach of Na'ama Bay and extends to the beach where it operates a cafeteria and an oriental tent which offers a variety of local herbal teas including *helba* (fenugreek), *irfa* (cinnamon), and *ganzabeel* (ginger). The space-age bubbles in front of the hotel are cheaper than the rooms in the main building and are comfortable and air-conditioned, sleeping two or three. Dinner in the restaurant is U.S. $10.50, LE 12.50 for Egyptians. Major credit cards accepted. Reservations: (062) 770175 or via Sharm el-Sheikh operator ext. 768; direct Cairo line: 768385. Cairo reservations: Sinai Hotels and Diving Clubs, 32 Sabry Abu Alam, P.O. Box 2336. Telephone: 3930200/3930301/3931543. Telex: 94002 OHTEG UN.

(B) Sanafir: This delightful hotel opened in September 1987 and has been fully booked ever since—to get a room you have to ask repeatedly if there are any cancellations, but even then you'll probably be unlucky. Rooms are simply but tastefully decorated, or you can stay in a Bedouin-style straw hut for two for about half the price. The bar serves cocktails and (rare in Sinai, for some reason) fresh lemon juice, and the restaurant (LE 15) is celebrated by those who like eating as much as they like diving. No credit cards. Sanafir camel trips include (per person) a U.S. $25 day trip or a U.S. $55 overnight trip into the mountains inclusive of camel,

guide, and food, or a U.S. $125 three-night excursion to St. Catherine's by camel and four-wheel-drive vehicle. Two days' notice is required for a party of more than four. Reservations: Sharm el-Sheikh operator ext. 551. Telex: 66036 HISHK UN (attn Sanafir).

(B) Aquamarine: Due to reopen in March 1990. Dinner is served in the Wrecker's Den Restaurant (LE 15, or U.S. $10 for foreigners). Major credit cards accepted. The Aquamarine is also a diving club. Reservations: (062) 770474. Cairo reservations: Pullman International, 9 Menes Street, Korba, Heliopolis. Telephone: 2908802/2908804/660249/679577. Telex: 21995 WAGON UN.

(C) Gafy Camp: Rented tents are available including breakfast and one cup of tea (an extra cup costs 50 piasters). Chalets are also available. Sweet water is turned on three times a day, but this is of academic interest as the showers are very temperamental. A fun place for young people, but not for tired campers as the disco goes on until the early hours and the late bus to Cairo careers cheerfully round the compound at midnight, horn blaring. Trips can be arranged by jeep (U.S. $10) and boat (U.S. $20) to include lunch and snorkeling gear. Reservations: Sharm el-Sheikh operator ext. 608. Cairo reservations: 2902090.

(C) Mersa Elaat Camping: Mersa Elaat or El'At, as the area was known before the Israelis called it Na'ama Bay, is the name adopted for this campsite run by the Sharm el-Sheikh City Council. Although it looks rather dismal the camp is well organized, but language problems may be encountered. There is an area for barbecues and washing-up, sites for campfires, and (cold) sweet water runs all day long in the shower rooms. No restaurant, but a shop sells mineral water, cold drinks, and canned food. Charges vary according to whether you rent a tent or bring your own.

Restaurants

Sanafir: The decor is resort-rustic, the food excellent, and the talk wafting from the other tables is all about moray eels and dive charts. The menu changes daily, but typically includes soup or salad, tuna steaks or lobster, and an exciting sorbet. The set dinner is LE 18, lobster is extra.

Wrecker's Den: The bar and furniture in the Aquamarine's delightfully ramshackle restaurant were built of timbers from an old wreck. Fish menu, LE 6.

See also Clifftop Hotel and Sandy Palace Restaurant, Sharm el-Sheikh.

Na'ama Bay to Dahab and Assalah (90 kms)

Dive sites along this route:

Near and Middle Coral Gardens (389 kms from Suez)
Tiger Bay (371 kms)
The Canyon (374 kms)
Wichita Falls (after 376 kms)
Ras Nasrani (after 376 kms)
el-Arkana (Nahalet el-Tel) (after 376 kms)
Maria Schröder (after 376 kms)
Shora el-Manqata (after 376 kms)
Ras Atantur (after 376 kms)

At **368 kms** from Suez: Leave Na'ama Bay.
- **369 kms:** A paved road on the right leads to the Suez Canal University Marine Studies Institute. At the top, just inside the gate, you can obtain the best view of Na'ama Bay.

Near and Middle Coral Gardens: The coral gardens are three shallow dives, of which two are close together and the third only accessible by boat. They are mostly visited by boat and seen as drift dives; in this way you can see two in one dive. You can walk here over the rocks from Na'ama Bay, but not with your diving gear.

For access from the road, turn left off the road leading up to the institute onto a well-marked track just before the gate. This is a rough ride only suitable for vehicles with four-wheel drive. The track winds about and you need to scout your way to the dive site entrances: Near Garden is almost on the corner of Na'ama Bay, a little sandy beach with a low, flat, overhanging rock which marks the entry. To get to the Middle Garden is even more difficult. You will have to drive back a little way, then turn north—the track is quite clear, but it is just as tough as it looks. Middle Garden, again, is on a sandy beach, secluded and perfect for camping. You can loop back without going all the way to Near Garden.

The beautifully sculptured gardens are well worth the slight trouble of reaching them. You might see rays or sharks here, but look out for small creatures, nudibranchs and so on.

It is not possible to continue from here to Far Garden, in fact this site can be reached only by boat.

All the shoreline from here until Ras Nasrani is sandy-bottomed, and therefore unsuitable for diving in windy weather or for divers who are inexperienced and might stir up the sand, drastically reducing visibility. Because of the sandy bottom the area abounds in manta, spotted, eagle, and tiger rays which feed on mollusks in the sand.

371 kms: Tiger Bay.

Tiger Bay: A track off to the right, at first suitable for ordinary cars, leads after about 2 kilometers to a demolished Israeli army camp. With the tangled wire and stone blocks just ahead of you, take the left fork and keep going until you are opposite the southern tip of Tiran Island (leased by Egypt from Saudi Arabia). You will see two beaches below; both can be reached by four-wheel drive (without a trailer). Enter from either of the sandy slopes. On the left side you will find broken corals and some good caves, and on the right a slope down to 60 meters. The beach makes a good place for camping and picnicking, and while you are waiting for the kettle to boil you can explore the gullies around for plants and fossilized shells. From higher ground, clearly visible on the horizon through binoculars, the wrecks of the *Lara* and the *Lulia* lie on the reef.

374 kms: The Canyon.

The Canyon: A continuation of a canyon that slips down through the cliff into the sea; home of a desalination project, the Canyon can clearly be seen from the road. The track is sandy and a four-wheel-drive vehicle would be needed to carry heavy gear, but an ordinary vehicle might make it if driven with care. The Canyon (not to be confused with the Canyon at Dahab) has a suitable slope for teaching courses, falling to some depth.

376 kms: T-junction. Continue straight ahead to Nasrani Airport and Nabq (16 kilometers), and left to Dahab (84 kilometers). If you have a four-wheel-drive vehicle you will be able to carry on to the Dahab road by branching left through the Wadi Ghomr at Ras Atantur (40 kilometers); if not, you must come all the way back here in order to continue your northward journey.

The dives in the Nabq area are all shallow, from 12 to 15 meters, and as the bottom tends to be sandy you can only get the most out of your dive if you avoid bad weather. To reach the sites, take the road to the airport. Ask the Bedouin for directions if you have difficulty in locating any of the sites.

At **1 km** from the junction: The track off to the right, parallel to the airport fence, leads to Wichita Falls. Head left and continue along the track down the cliff. Wichita Falls can only be reached by four-wheel drive, without a trailer; there is no anchor for boats. There is a sandy slope at the entrance. Here you should see big groupers as well as the beautiful corals and abundant marine life visible all along this stretch. It is also a good area for night diving.

4 kms: Ras Nasrani Airport. Along this part of the coast are several sheltered camping spots, the most popular of which is Nasrani beach. After passing the airport peel off to the right, round the perimeter fence, and keep going for several kilometers along the sand track until you arrive at the beach. Avoid it on crowded weekends when it can become unpleasant, if not unhygienic.

Ras Nasrani: Enter the water from the beach, taking care because of the deep sand. This is an excellent site for drift dives by boat, and for night dives.

8.5 kms: MFO camp, surrounded by fenced-in minefields.

10 kms: You draw level with the wrecks of the *Lara* and the *Lulia,* the former poised on the Gordon reef.

12.5 kms: Two more stranded wrecks. One is the Israeli *Hey Dorama,* a water carrier which used to bring water from Eilat to Sharm el-Sheikh, parked on the reef in protest in 1967, when President Nasser sealed off the Straits of Tiran and prevented Israel from reaching the Red Sea. The other is half a Greek freighter "wrecked" for an insurance claim.

15 kms: A microwave tower.

17.5 kms: Nabq. Ministry of Interior (*shurta dakhiliya*) soldiers at the checkpoint will register your passport. A track to the NW leads over the mountains to the main road.

21.5 kms: el-Arkana (Nahalet el-Tel).

El-Arkana (Nahalet el-Tel): A trail of mangroves stretches out to sea on the southern edge of a shallow bay. You pass a group of small huts and a grove of palm trees which makes a pretty camping site. Enter the water anywhere, crossing the mud to reach the beautiful channels and lagoons among the reef patches. This site is just as exciting for snorkelers as for divers.

25 kms: Mangroves cluster on the north of the bay. Through them you can see the rusting hull of the *Maria Schröder,* resting on the reef ever since she was put there during a storm in 1965. Again, this is a pretty camping place—but please don't leave any litter!

Maria Schröder: You can reach the ship and enter for a dive only by crossing the small lagoon just north of the mangroves and to the left of the wreck, but the sea can be rough here so you must only attempt it in calm weather.

31 kms: A grove of palms marks the junction of several tracks. On the left, a road runs to the Sharm el-Sheikh–Dahab highway. Ahead, a lush mangrove swamp, the last on this coast and the most northerly in the world.

Shora el-Manqata: Just before the mangrove swamp you will reach a flat sand strip jutting into the sea between two blue lagoons. Enter the water on the left side of the sandspit and dive round to the right.

Continuing along the track you will soon see the dark flanks of Ras Atantur with a police post below, and behind a sweep of massive, inhospitable bluffs along the edge of which a road once ran to Dahab but which is now blocked by rockfalls. Through binoculars you can see the southern oasis of Dahab.

40.5 kms: Police checkpoint at the place known variously as Halayib, Halaba, or Wadi Ghomr—again, your passport will be registered.

Ras Atantur: This, the last of the Sharm el-Sheikh dives, is straight ahead past the checkpoint. Stop at the end of the track and enter here—this is a moderately deep dive of 20 to 30 meters. Turn to the left to explore the virgin reef, disturbed only by Bedouin lobster fishers.

Unless you have a four-wheel-drive vehicle you must now retrace your route to the Ras Nasrani T-junction. With four-wheel drive—or a Peugeot—you can reach the main Sharm el-Sheikh–Dahab road 12.5 kilometers away by turning off just past the police checkpoint, before Ras Atantur, along the rocky road of loose pink and black granite stones through the Wadi Ghomr.

Wadi Ghomr

At **376 kms** from Suez: At the Dahab–Ras Nasrani T-junction, turn left for Dahab. In front lies a wide sandy plain which runs from the mountains down to the cliff face behind you. There is almost no sign of life, but in the valleys ahead you will pass scattered Bedouin settlements where traditional black goat-hair tents have been largely replaced by huts built of any material that comes to hand, and a pickup truck has as likely as not taken over from the camel as a convenient form of transport. Camels still play an important economic role in Bedouin life, however, and you should keep a lookout for them as they are apt to wander all over the road.

406 kms: A track on the right leads to Nabq. If you are trying to reach Nabq on your own for the first time you would be well advised to take the road from Nasrani mentioned above (at the 376-kilometer point) and to find the way back from Nabq to this point along the main road, imprinting it on your mind for future reference. This might, however, be an inconvenience if you are attempting to reach Nabq from Dahab and wish to avoid making a 30-kilometer detour. Remember the coastal track is passable only as far as Ras Atantur: do not attempt to continue towards Dahab. Any of the dive centers in Na'ama Bay will help you to arrange a guided jeep trip to Nabq.

416 kms: Scrawled on the back of a yellow and black road sign just after a steep curve in the road is the word SCUBA (this faces south—if you're coming from Dahab you'll have to look back to see it). This marks the end of the track to Ras Atantur through the pass of the Wadi Ghomr, which can clearly be seen running towards the sea. Another sign on the main road at this end of the track demands No Trespassing.

The beautiful barren mountains you are passing through were formed during the early Proterozoic era, between 15 hundred million and 6 hundred million years ago. They are old and craggy, and any fossils on them were weathered away long ago. Their colors demonstrate their volcanic origin: they have, so to speak, been put through the mangle. What appears to be bedding or jointing is often the mark of a contorted lava flow. The layers in the rocks are dikes: cracks in the cooled rocks filled up with later material. The colors are caused by the uplifting of land to form mountains, the metamorphosis of rocks, and the concentration of minerals. This valley is today a wadi—hence the rocks strewn along the bottom with colors which correspond to the patches of mineralization higher up in the mountains. The sharp gradient of the rocks on either side tells us that this was once an ancient shoreline. The bottoms of the rocks are truncated, and not typical of a wadi created by flash floods.

432.5 kms: Shahira Pass: The highest point on the road between Sharm el-Sheikh and Dahab is marked by a squat obelisk of red granite stones, erected in memory of an Israeli colonel who was killed during the 1973 war when his jeep hit a land mine. The wrecked jeep lies at the foot of the obelisk. Local Bedouin say the colonel haunts the spot, taking a short walk in the early morning.

The rock colors are particularly vibrant at this spot, which makes a convenient resting place. Part of the area is still fenced off with wire, which means it is probably mined.

441.5 kms: The main road ascends a slight incline and drops down a gentle slope. On the gravelly plain at the bottom, a track can clearly be seen tucking itself round the mountain. This is the track through the Wadi Qnai to the coast at the Southern Oasis (see below after 461 kilometers), a beautiful camping and swimming area south of Dahab. The track soon becomes so sandy that a four-wheel-drive vehicle is necessary: if you have one, don't miss the opportunity to see this wadi, which runs through a dike-streaked yellow sandstone gorge reminiscent of the Siq at Petra. When it meets the sea at the Southern Oasis you will see palm trees lining the beach, and the Egyptian flag waving over a police station. If you want to dive or camp drive over to the checkpoint to register your passport. To reach Dahab from this point, drive through the wire fence of the old kibbutz (on the left as you approach the

Wadi Qnai, Dahab

village) or across the mud flats around the perimeter fence of
the holiday village (on your right).

450 kms: The road swings right on its approach to Dahab as the
mountains, which have been hugging the shore, pull away
from the sea.

456 kms: T-junction. Turn left to Nuweiba and St. Catherine's,
right to Dahab.

459 kms: Dahab.

Dahab

You have now entered the wide coastal plain of Dahab, at the
mouth of several wadis. It stretches from the Bedouin village of
Assalah in the north to the Southern Oasis at the mouth of Wadi
Qnai, with the holiday village, the administrative village, and
the MFO contained in their own little pockets between the two.
On your left, near a small police post, a track sweeps round the
headland to a 10-kilometer stretch of coral reef for divers and
snorkelers to explore, culminating in the famous Blue Hole (see
below). If you turn right at the shore you come to a tarmac road
which leads to Assalah village (see below). The main road
continues on to the holiday village and draws to a halt at a
helicopter pad; the other sections of the delta are reached by
their own roads or tracks.

Dive sites
The track runs to the left from the main road down to the sea, and
turns north round the headland. It is well used and suitable for
all vehicles.

The Canyon: After following the track for 8 kilometers you
will find yourself at the Canyon, marked by a half-built
restaurant on the southern side of the cliff. If you stand with
your back to the restaurant and look on your right-hand side
you will see that the entrance to this spectacular dive site,
one of the best in the area, is through a blue lagoon which
interrupts the reef. Snorkel through the lagoon (it is often
windy here, and difficult to snorkel over the reef table). Exit
from the right-hand side of the lagoon, through a break in the
coral, and turn north until you are opposite the cliff face; at
exactly 18 meters you will see a pinnacle, and below it a hole.
The hole descends to 48 meters: there are two exits, the first at
30 meters and the second at the end. Only advanced divers

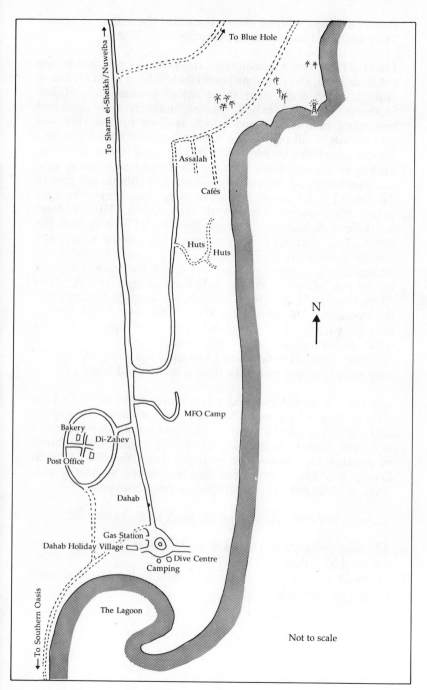

Dahab and Assalah

should attempt to enter the Canyon; for the less experienced there are lots of surrounding pinnacles to explore.

The Blue Hole: Two kilometers on from the Canyon, just before the Blue Hole, the road has been blocked by a rockfall. Leave your car and walk over the blocked promontory, Nakeb Shaheen, formerly called Gamal Shaheen after a camel belonging to one Shaheen which walked up the cliff and unfortunately fell off it. Two hundred meters ahead you will see the Blue Hole, visible as a deep blue pool in the coral reef. This is an unforgettable spot for divers and snorkelers, who can snorkel round the rim of the hole (the submerged part of the rim is 1 to 1.3 meters below the surface) and enjoy the most vivid displays of coral and reef fishes. Divers (and snorkelers) should enter through the channel leading from the beach. This channel is very narrow, but can be seen quite clearly somewhat to the right of the center of the hole. Alternatively, snorkel around the reef table from the point where you left your car. The hole itself plunges to a depth of 80 meters. At 62 meters is an archway through the reef into the open sea. This is a deep, dangerous dive which should only be attempted by advanced divers, and only at midday when the overhead sun shines directly into the hole. All equipment and dive tables must be carefully checked here; it's easy to be forgetful when the dive is so rich and beautiful.

Ras Abu Galuum: A one and a half hour's walk from the Blue Hole on foot or by camel. There is a beach suitable for camping and a dive site—not a great one, although the fish population is varied. Camels, essential to carry diving gear, can be hired at Assalah (see below) or arranged from the dive club in Dahab. Ras Abu Galuum can also be reached by four-wheel-drive vehicles from the main road, or from Nuweiba.

Retrace your route back along the track to the main road.

At **459 kms** from Suez: The track leading to the Canyon rejoins the road to Dahab.
461 kms: A tarmac road on the left leads to the Bedouin oasis village of Assalah.

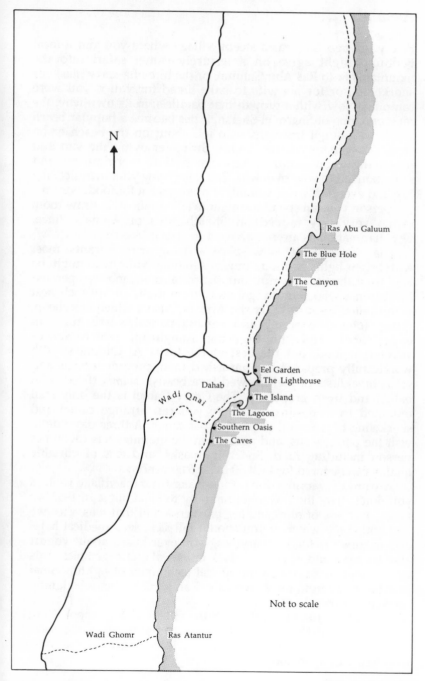

Dahab dive sites

Assalah

Five years ago this was a sleepy village where you and a local Bedouin might agree on a leisurely camel safari into the mountains or to Ras Abu Galuum, or the hire of a leaky mask for snorkeling, or for his wife to bake bread for you if you were camping. Now with a growth that parallels, in its own way, the mushrooming of Sharm el-Sheikh, it has become a popular beach resort for budget travelers, who loll about on the beach or on Assalah's version of the "Sunset Strip," enjoying the sun and practicing their Arabic. Accommodation is primitive and sanitation left to your own wits. You must bring your own sleeping bag and everything else you might need, except for food. For LE 2 per person you can spend the night in a Bedouin-style straw room (often very tiny indeed) at Sheikh Ali's or Awda's Place. Egyptian nationals are not allowed to stay in Assalah.

The "Sunset Strip" now sports a string of restaurants, most with bright lights and loud music. Although your meal might be held up if the butagaz runs out, the restaurants, mostly operated by Cairenes who want to "get away from it all," do try their best with limited resources. Try the African Queen, which has cheap, filling food (the honey and banana pancakes are quite an experience), and the Fighting Kangaroo, which serves vegetarian food, but the best of the lot is Al Capone's, with wonderfully prepared and garnished food, prompt service, and great breakfasts of *foul* (stewed fava beans), *taamia* (fried bean balls), and fresh grapefruit. The Crazy Camel is the only stall operated by Bedouins, and here you can arrange camel and snorkeling trips for LE 15 per day per camel. A three-day ride to visit the pools, wells, and gardens in the mountains is LE 50 per person including food. Snorkels, masks, and fins of variable quality can be hired for LE 4.50 to LE 5.00 per day.

A word of warning: don't drink water from the village well, as you don't share the Bedouin immunity to Sinai bugs. In 1982 we nearly lost one of our camping partners—and that was after we had boiled the water. If you should fall sick, seek medical help, and meanwhile forget everything you ever heard about yogurt and dry toast and, if you can, tuck into meat and vegetables. This rather singular advice on the special techniques of fighting Sinai diarrhea came from the young American MFO medics who kindly revived our friend.

The tarmac road runs through the village to the school. Here it becomes a dirt track and continues to the north of the oasis where it hits the sea and joins the track leading from the main road to the Canyon and the Blue Hole.

Dive sites

The Lighthouse: In the middle of the village of Assalah, the lighthouse (look for a pylon with a box on top) marks the entrance of the dive site. Enter on the right of the lighthouse and proceed round to the left. This is a medium–shallow dive around the reef wall.

Eel Garden: You can carry on to here on your Lighthouse dive and double back, or you can enter from the northernmost date palms of the village, just round the corner from the lighthouse. A shallow dive with an eel garden.

461 kms: Soon after the road leading to Assalah, on the right, is a sign marked el-Masharaba Tourist Village. This is the former Israeli settlement of Di-Zahev vacated in 1982 after the settlers had destroyed their plantations and uprooted the date palms they had planted on the beach. This is one way to the Southern Oasis dive site; the other is to drive round the perimeter fence of the holiday village. Enter the settlement— now housing local employees—through a gate in the barbed-wire fence and continue inside the perimeter, passing a bakery on your left. Turn right at the crossroads (if you go straight ahead you will come to the "city hall" and the post office). Keep right, and take the track leading out of the camp and turning right along the edge of the lagoon. You pass a camel police post on your right.

The track is smooth, solid, and easily accessible to cars, but the ride is marred by the line of dirty rubbish along the high-water mark and the ubiquitous windblown plastic bags caught on the bushes. After 7.5 kilometers you reach a pretty oasis with a notice in Arabic, English, and Hebrew put up by the Ministry of the Interior advising against photography. Blocking the track is a police checkpoint. You must show your passport before being allowed through, and you must ask here for permission if you want to camp for the night—and also warn the guards, who are entitled to shoot on sight at night, if you wish to go night diving (or swimming). Drive to the end of the oasis, decorated with more plastic bags, for your dives.

Dive sites

Southern Oasis: The Southern Oasis makes a tranquil camping site, with some shelter from the wind provided by the date palms. I have slept in the open here in late November. The entrance to the dive site is at the point of the furthest date palm, and the access is easier at high tide. Snorkel over the reef and proceed some yards out to sea where the sandy slope drops to more than 40 meters. Turn right and circle back to the shallow reef. There is a sandy bottom with small pinnacles inhabited by sea horses, nudibranchs, Spanish dancers, and other small creatures usually seen at night, and many soft corals.

The Caves: Considered by many a more interesting dive than the Southern Oasis. Keep going round the bay until you reach the second of two stone cairns near the waterline, opposite a deep cleft in the cliff face, where a patch of sand marks the entrance to the Caves. Keep to the left, where you will encounter an eel garden.

The road carries on twisting round the shoreline at the foot of the mountains, which seem to be falling into the sea. A car can negotiate the track, though one with a high clearance or four-wheel drive would make the journey less precarious. The track used to go all the way to Ras Atantur and on to Nabq (see Nabq, above) but is now blocked by rockfalls.

If you are in a four-wheel-drive vehicle you can reach the Sharm el-Sheikh–Nuweiba highway by turning right at the police station and driving through the Wadi Qnai (see above, p.82).

Accommodation

Dahab Holiday Village: Retrace your route through the Southern Oasis and the old kibbutz to reach the lagoon. If you turn right at the main road you will soon come to the holiday complex run by the Pullman International hotel chain.

The Israeli-built hotel is air-conditioned, but in the bathrooms a water barrel and bucket are needed to help you cope with low water pressure. As guests have little choice but to use the hotel restaurant (unless they wish to eat in Assalah), they must pay half or full board.

Sturdy bamboo huts are also available at cheap rates, but the shared toilets are filthy and the showers don't work. The hotel has a pleasant beach for which a fee of LE 1 is charged to nonguests, and where sailboards and pedalos can be hired. The lagoon in front of the hotel is an excellent location for experienced windsurfers—there may be too much wind for beginners. Reservations: (062) 770788. Cairo reservations: Pullman International, 9 Menes Street, Korba, Heliopolis. Telephone: 2908802/2908804/660249/679577. Telex: 21995 WAGON UN.

In front of the hotel are the bus station and car park, including a helicopter landing pad, and a gas station is next door. The cafeteria on the corner sells beer.

Dive centers
The Diving Centre opens from 8:30 A.M. to 6:00 P.M.; hire prices are similar to those in Na'ama Bay: for example U.S. $35 (Egyptian nationals may pay in Egyptian pounds) for a two-dive day, and U.S. $175 for a two-star CMS or NAUI course. The equipment, though, is rather less reliable. Sailboards can be hired. Contact the Cairo office for courses: minimum three, maximum eight people.

Dive sites
The Lagoon: Conveniently situated right in front of the Diving Centre, this is a dive less abundant in marine life than most of the other Dahab dives. The visibility below 10 meters is poor.

Napoleon Reef: This is a boat dive (arrangements can be made with the Diving Centre). As the name suggests, napoleon (humphead wrasse) are often to be seen.

The Island: The site is to be found 2 kilometers along the coast from the Diving Centre, before Assalah village. The "island" is only a little way offshore; anyone in the village will help you to locate it.

Retrace your route to the Sharm el-Sheikh–Nuweiba road.

Dahab to Nuweiba (74 kms)

At **456 kms** from Suez: Junction with the road from Sharm el-Sheikh. Continue straight ahead for St. Catherine's Monastery and Nuweiba.

460 kms: On the right-hand side of the road is a classic example of concurrent thick bands of black dikes cutting through the pink granite rocks.

464 kms: The road leaves a major wadi and crosses a pass into a valley flanked by miniature limestone cliffs clinging at a slanted angle to the slopes of much older rocks. Unlike many of the surrounding hills they have survived the tough weathering of the desert, and the slanting bedding lines of the mountains, once penetrated by an equatorial sea, show some movement in recent earth history. Dark debris from the older igneous rock lies scattered like burnt breadcrumbs on the creamy limestone.

473 kms: On the left of the wadi, pockets of white sand are the only visible remnants of once-flourishing ancient reefs in what is now a river valley.

494 kms: The turnoff to St. Catherine's (86 kms).

501 kms: A panoramic view stretches ahead across the remaining mountains of south Sinai as the road begins its descent. There are bends and sharp gradients to watch out for, but clear warnings are posted. Coasting is prohibited.

Lying about are large boulders that could not be moved without considerable force such as that generated by the torrents that rush through a wadi where the gradient is so steep.

518 kms: The road reaches the coast. Below lies the oasis of Nuweiba, fringing a long bay.

Nuweiba

Like Dahab, Nuweiba lies in a wide delta carved by the flash floods of several adjoining wadis. At the southern end of the delta lies the Sayadin Beach Hotel and the port with its Aqaba-bound ferry. At the northern end, the town of Nuweiba, the tourist village, and the Bedouin settlement of Terabien. Dotted about the plain are umbrella-shaped *saayil* trees (acacias), much loved by camels who reach up to browse on the upper branches. On the other side of the gulf, the mountains of Saudi Arabia shift their colors from hazy red to purple.

At the time of writing, there are no compressors or other diving facilities in Nuweiba.

518 kms: On the right is the turnoff to the Sayadin Beach Hotel, set in the Muzeina Oasis which in spite of its palms and vegetation has no water sweet enough to drink. It is inhabited by the Muzeina tribe who reached Sinai from Saudi Arabia and settled widely in the peninsula's eastern half—Assalah, near Dahab, is also a Muzeina village. The Muzeina are occupied largely in small farming projects and in catering to tourists rather than in "trading," the rather more lucrative pursuit of many of their neighbors. From the oasis an unpaved road runs along the coast as far as Ras Abu Galuum, which swimmers and snorkelers will find worth exploring in a four-

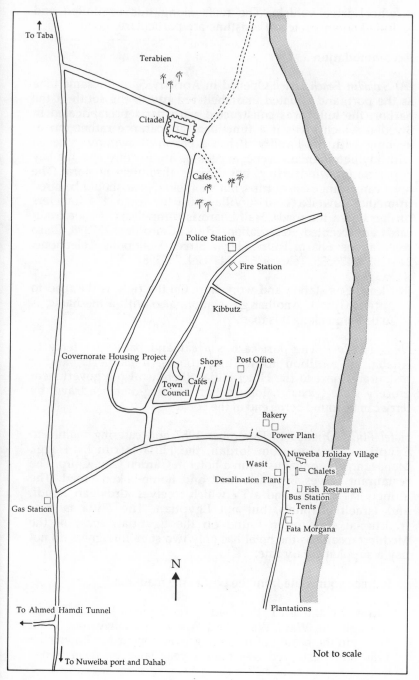

To Taba

Terabien

Citadel

Cafés

Police Station

Fire Station

Kibbutz

Governorate Housing Project

Shops

Post Office

Town Council

Cafés

Bakery

Power Plant

Nuweiba Holiday Village

Wasit

Chalets

Desalination Plant

Fish Restaurant

Bus Station

Tents

Fata Morgana

Gas Station

N

To Ahmed Hamdi Tunnel

Plantations

Not to scale

To Nuweiba port and Dahab

Nuweiba

wheel-drive vehicle. The reefs along this unspoiled and little-known stretch of coastline are particularly good.

Accommodation

(A) Sayadin Beach Hotel: Opened in April 1985, at the same time as the port, and situated in a sheltered bay to the south of the harbor, the hotel was constructed with parts prefabricated in Sweden which gives it a functional appearance rather out of keeping with the locality. It has a beautiful swimming beach with idyllic mountain scenery; pedalos are for hire and the bay is perfect for windsurfing, but there is absolutely no coral. The hotel can arrange camel trips, but snorkeling gear should be hired from the Nuweiba Tourist Village (in the town, 8 kilometers further down the road). Half board is compulsory. Major credit cards are accepted. Reservations: direct Cairo line: 757398. Cairo reservations: Sharm Tours, Hegaz Street, Heliopolis. Telephone: 2454183/2476535. Telex: 92634 AIT UN. 757398.

520 kms: Gas station and workshop. On the right is the road to Nuweiba port. Another gas station, also with a mechanic, is to be found along this road.

Nuweiba Port: The port carries a car and passenger ferry to Aqaba. In addition to waiting rooms, a cafeteria, and a restaurant (next to the Hotel Flifla), there is also a government grocery store *(gamaia)*. Information on long-distance travel by ferry can be found at the end of the book.

Hotel Flifla: Opened in December 1987 and catering mainly to Egyptians arriving from Jordan, the Flifla is run by Hagga Mahazan, who previously ran a hotel in Garden City, Cairo. The restaurant serves Egyptian food and home-baked bread. The lounge has a video and a TV which receives Jordanian, Saudi, and Israeli channels, but not Egyptian. The Flifla is in a traditional style often found on the Egyptian coast of the Mediterranean. As the hotel has only two stars foreigners do not pay a supplementary rate.

Retrace your route from the port to the main road.

523 kms: On the left is the road to the Ahmed Hamdi Tunnel through the Wadi Watir and Ain Furtaga, rivaling Wadi Feiran in the beauty of its palm groves. Opened in November 1986 and destroyed less than a year later by flash floods which swept away cars and buses and took several lives, this road was nevertheless rebuilt within five months.

526 kms: Just before entering the northern oasis you reach a crossroads. On the left is a gas station with a papyrus bazaar and a restaurant catering by arrangement to passing tour groups, although individual travelers will have to go to the Nuweiba Tourist Village for a meal. The right-hand turn leads to the town of Nuweiba and the holiday village run by the Sinai Company for Hotels and Diving Clubs.

To reach the town, turn right at the gas station and then left. Almost immediately you come to a road junction. The road on the left leads past a municipal housing project and on to the village of Terabien; halfway along is a bazaar selling local handicrafts run by Rima, the Swiss wife of a Bedouin guide. Straight ahead lies the city council building housing a public international telephone, medical and dental clinics, and a government grocery store (*gamaia*). On the right of the council building are some cafeterias and a barber, and behind these a street with some small shops selling groceries and post cards. Follow this street, which runs along one side of the old Israeli settlement, and take the third turning on the left to reach the post office where mail may be sent and collected. Retrace your steps out of the town to reach the main road.

Leaving the town, turn left towards Wasit, the central coastal strip. On the left, in front of a power station, you will see a gray shed: this is the local bakery, which bakes very good bread (ask there for baking times). The road now curves to the right.

Nuweiba Tourist Village: Set in spacious gardens of hibiscus and oleander, the village bungalows vary between the old Israeli-built hotel rooms with erratic plumbing and the new rooms with solar-powered water heaters. All rooms are pleasantly furnished. The restaurant serves breakfast and table-d'hôte lunch and dinner, and the fish restaurant, which opens every evening at eight and is to be found beyond the chalets to the left of the hotel, serves locally caught seafood for LE 12 per person.

On the hotel beach, alongside the bar and disco, an open-air restaurant serves barbecues and kebabs. To one side of this is an oriental tent where you can smoke a water pipe and sample Bedouin coffee and tea. The beach can be very windy, either in the morning or in the afternoon, depending on the time of year, so choose a sturdy screen to shelter behind for sunbathing. The coral off the beach is very pretty. Snorkeling equipment, a glass-bottomed boat, and sailboards can be hired on the beach from the Diving Centre, which, strictly speaking, does not function as such and has no compressor. The hotel is a meeting point for the South Sinai Travel Agency, which arranges camel safaris from Na'ama Bay. Prices vary between the old wings and the new one, which has a constant supply of solar-heated water. The set lunch is LE 11.00, dinner LE 12.50. Major credit cards are accepted. Reservations: (062) 770393; direct Cairo line: 768832. Cairo reservations: Sinai Hotels and Diving Clubs, 32 Sabry Abu Alam, P.O. Box 2336. Telephone: 3930200/3930301/3931543. Telex: 94002 OHTEG UN.

Almost opposite the gate to the tourist village is a desalination plant which processes water for the Nuweiba area. On the left, a short road leads to the back of the tourist village, its fish restaurant, and the bus station (where there is a taxi stand for local and long-distance service). Near the bus station are several tents which can be rented from the village. The next track on the left leads to the Fata Morgana fish restaurant and cafeteria.

Further along the road passes another former Israeli settlement, egg and chicken farms, and several market gardens and plantations. The floods which swept through Nuweiba in 1987 caused considerable damage to this part of the delta.

At **526 kms** from Suez: The gas station and crossroads. Just north from the gas station a road on the right leads to Terabien, the

Turkish citadel, Nuweiba

Bedouin settlement of largely new, one-story houses set in the northern oasis, where, except for mountain cisterns, the last supply of natural drinking water is to be found before Taba. Dominating the village is a small citadel built by the Turks in the eighteenth century. The village, which may yet become as crowded as Assalah, has a few cafeterias aimed at tourists: the Fish and Chip Restaurant and the Palm Beach. A track runs through the village and north along the coast; a hot, desolate stretch with a stony beach where a private tourist complex is under construction.

Nuweiba to Taba (63 kms)

Accommodation along this route:

Basata (549 kms)
Sally Land Tourist Village (554 kms)

Dive sites along this route:

Devil's Head (538 kms)
Big Ruta (542 kms)
Ras el-Burqa and Coral Garden (549 kms)
Mersa el-Muqabila (571 kms)
Sun Pool (578 kms)
Pharaoh's Island (581 kms)

Leaving the sleepy, sandy village of Terabien the road now hugs the coast for most of the way to Taba. If the water invites you in for a swim or a snorkel, simply pull up your car and go in. But beware entering the water on rocky beaches when the wind is blowing and the sea is a little rough; these are tiring conditions for swimming. And be sure to leave the beach at night. There are few places secluded enough to camp along here, but if you do find a cove where you'd like to pitch your tent you should ask permission from the police at Nuweiba, Ras el-Burqa (at 549 kilometers from Suez), or Pharaoh's Island (at 581 kilometers). At intervals you may see fishermen along the shore, and camels foraging on the roadside. It's perfectly all right to offer the camels your leftover picnic (they often hang about outside the bakery waiting for tidbits) but according to Bedouin lore you must not succumb to the temptation to give them a drink of water: this is considered to be enticement, and tantamount to stealing.

At **536 kms** from Suez: The road cuts through the rocks at Margena. By arrangement a Bedouin guide can take you up into these mountains to see the Blue Canyon (painted blue in the late 1970s by the Belgian artist Jean Verame), the Painted Canyon colored with natural stone, and the cisterns of Wishwashi, where you can plunge into a natural swimming pool of clear sweet water.

The road is approaching the Devil's Head, a dive site at a small rocky cape. Looking north along the beach, the cape seems to resemble a sinister face turning towards you, but this cannot be seen from the road. The stretch of beach to the south of this promontory is good for swimming, but unfortunately is littered with bottles and tin cans. It would be a great service to the Sinai if tourists could be persuaded to take their litter home with them.

538 kms: *Devil's Head.* If you think you may have missed the head, look out for a small cafeteria on the left-hand side of the road. Now look back, and you will see the rock. Drive along the track leading off the road, and park near a large white notice warning against swimming. Don't swim here, on the north side of the cape: if you look in the water you can see a strong riptide. Sadly the beach is littered with rubbish and broken glass, most of it with Israeli labels. Climb on to the rock to map out your dive. In spite of the notice, the entrance for the dive is immediately to the north of the rock, so take care not to attempt this in bad weather. Continue around the reef, exiting from the small blue lagoon to the south, and be prepared to encounter sharks. There is too much rubbish for one to be tempted to linger on the beach.

542 kms: The Starko campsite, in a prize position on a good swimming beach.

Near here is an offshore reef patch with a wreck known as *Big Ruta,* which can only be visited by boat. This can be arranged from Basata (see below). Diving facilities in the vicinity are limited at present.

549 kms: Basata at Ras el-Burqa

Basata: A police post marks the incline down to the campsite. On the left, the words of a popular patriotic song: سينا رجعت كاملة لينا (Sinai has come back to us in one piece) are spelled out in white pebbles. Basata, which in Arabic means "simplicity," is owned and run by Sherif el-Ghamrawy, an engineer by profession. It provides upmarket beach camping in what is less a campsite than an exercise in community living, with an emphasis on Bedouin manners and customs. Guests can pitch their own tents or stay in Bedouin-style straw huts simply equipped with foam mattresses and rag rugs. The toilets—porcelain closets hand flushed with salt water—are kept scrupulously clean, and the showers, screened with rugs, follow the barrel-and-jug method with sweet water brought to the camp from the desalination plant at Nuweiba at a cost of LE 20 per cubic meter—so don't waste it. The large central tent is for communal cooking, dining, and relaxing. Here you can buy mineral water, milk and fruit juice, fresh vegetables, canned meat, and chocolate. The system is that you help yourself to food and make tea or coffee, then sign up for what you have used. A generator supplies electricity to the main areas. The camp is kept spotlessly clean and the atmosphere is friendly and welcoming. See Sherif if you want to make an excursion into the mountains or along the coast, or to hire a boat to visit the dive site of *Big Ruta*. Guests staying in huts are charged per person, with single occupants paying slightly more. Mastercard accepted. Write to Sherif el-Ghamrawy and Co., Basata, Ras el-Burqa, Nuweiba, South Sinai or telephone Amin Sami el-Ghamrawy, Cairo, telephone: 3501829.

Dive sites

Ras el-Burqa: The dive round this point at the north end of the beach, though shallow, is unspoilt and refreshing and the home of several moray eels. It is absolutely forbidden to climb up to the observatory on the top of Ras el-Burqa, at the northern end of the beach, though you may climb the sandy slopes on the north side of the observatory.

Coral Garden: This dive to the point on the right of the bay is more interesting. If you can interrupt your sunbathing on the sandy beach and snorkel round to it you will find a beautiful coral garden teeming with life. Drama is provided by an abundance of lionfish, so be careful, especially at dusk when the lionfish cluster into groups to surround their prey. The southern cliff here may be climbed.

A smooth, sandy swimming beach starts just after Ras el-Burqa and stretches close to the road for the next 13 kilometers. The shelf is steep, however, so swimmers should take reasonable care.

552 kms: Planned tourist project. Soon afterwards a notice prohibiting photography reminds one that there is another side to the Sinai than pleasure seeking. The border police have additional problems, and regularly patrol the beach for smuggling.

554 kms: Sally Land Tourist Village.

(B) *Sally Land Tourist Village:* With stone bungalows set in a small oasis, Sally Land was designed by owner/architect Zachariah Yehia and his American partner, John Harvie, and named for John's daughter. Only natural colors and materials have been used in its construction, so that the village is in harmony with its surroundings. The hotel, which opened in January 1988, is in a perfect situation for water sports—coral is to be found off the sandy beach—and for safaris to visit the mountain wells and oases. The restaurant serves Egyptian and American food, with homemade Bedouin bread and a fish smorgasbord. Windsurfing, sailing, fishing, and overnight dive trips are also available. One- to four-day safari trips can be arranged, costing LE 30 per day per camel, including food. Air-conditioned double rooms at Sally Land are good value. Reservations: Sally Land Tourist Village, Nuweiba, South Sinai. Cairo reservations: 743689 (evenings).

564 kms: The sandy coastline gives way to rocks, making entrance more difficult for snorkelers. The pebbly beach is difficult for ordinary vehicles, and there is no apparent interest to divers.
571 kms: Mersa el-Muqabila.

Mersa el-Muqabila: This famous dive site, marked by the usual Ministry of Interior notice prohibiting photography, is in a long bay banked by boulders and flanked by sandy beaches, the northern one being the most attractive for swimmers. This is an exciting dive: the entrance is from the northern corner of the bay, from where you can snorkel south-east to the center of the bay. At 20 meters are small caverns inhabited by octopuses, but visibility is poor.

Stone debris left by flash floods is strewn on either side of the road.
572 kms: The road leaves the coast and sweeps inland, rejoining the sea spectacularly after 6 kilometers where, if you glance back to the south, you will see a string of small sandy beaches; inviting, but quite inaccessible because there is no road.
578 kms: Sun Pool.

Sun Pool: Just on the left bend after the road rejoins the sea a white No Swimming notice on the shore marks the area of the Sun Pool, a miniature salt lake cut off from the sea by a raised stony beach. Drive round under the cliff on the south side of the headland, not over the mud flat which can be very soggy. The No Swimming notice, put there because of crosscurrents, marks, like the one at Devil's Head, the point where divers enter the water.

Turn left round the reef, diving to 12 meters. Around the corner is the shallow green Sun Pool, fringed by a thick bed of mud. If you have the courage to wade through it you can look for microscopic brown water fleas and other creatures.

579 kms: On the Taba road just north of the Sun Pool you will come to the Fjord, a turquoise blue inlet with steep cliffs. On top is the Salah el-Din restaurant run by the Nuweiba branch of the Sinai Hotels and Diving Clubs, where food is occasionally available. A Stella beer is LE 3.40, and soft drinks 80 piasters: no change can be tendered for large banknotes. You can make use of the toilet facilities, and park your car if you want to go down to the pretty swimming cove below.

580 kms: The road to the airport at Nakeb (22 kilometers), which follows the old pilgrim route from Nakhl through the Wadi Araba. The opening of the new road to the Ahmed Hamdi Tunnel and the international airport will make the north of the east coast much more accessible to tourism.

581 kms: Pharaoh's Island.

Pharaoh's Island: A small rocky island with a blue lagoon comes into sight. This natural fortress, for sharks, reefs, and high winds made its harbor virtually inaccessible to sailing vessels, was

The Fjord

used to advantage in the Byzantine era and probably much earlier. Salah el-Din captured the island in 1170 and built the present fortress from where, with the help of carrier pigeons which flew with messages to Cairo, he held the Crusaders at bay. At the same time he built Qal'at el-Gundi (Soldier's Fortress) in western Sinai (see p.51), in case the Crusaders managed to get that far. There is a story that in 1900 a British explorer found a tablet at Pharaoh's Island with detailed Arabic inscriptions which he was unfortunately unable to read, but that when an expedition returned some years later the stone appeared to have washed into the sea. However the fortress's date was determined during excavations and restoration by the Department of Antiquities. Whether the restoration has destroyed some of the romance of the island is a matter of personal taste, but the fortress is worth a visit. A boat runs to the island from the jetty below (fee LE 2).

A cafeteria on the island is run by the Misr–Sinai Tourist Company, but the supply of provisions is unreliable. If you wish to swim, snorkel, or dive round the island you can start from the jetty on the mainland or take the ferry and start on the other side; the dive is interesting, but unspectacular. You can expect to take about one and a half hours to circumnavigate the island, which is best attempted in an anticlockwise direction, and you need to be pretty fit and a good swimmer.

From here you have a panoramic view looking over the coasts of Saudi Arabia, Jordan, and Israel.

589 kms: Taba.

Taba

Doum palms cluster on the beach near the bus station. Here you can find a public international telephone and a *gamaia*, and, further along, the *(A) Hilton Hotel* (Reservations: direct Cairo line: 768200. Fax: (Cairo) 757152. Cairo reservations: Ramses Hilton, Nile Corniche. Telephone: 777444/768888, ext. 3144. Telex: 94260/94262/93930 HIRAM UN.).

If you are not an Egyptian national and have an Egyptian resident's or multiple-entry visa you can cross the border into Israel (leaving your car on the Egyptian side). If you do this, though, you will receive a Taba stamp in your passport which may cause difficulties if you want to travel elsewhere in the Arab world. (This applies, too, to any travelers entering Egypt through Taba.) If you are visiting Egypt on a tourist visa, however, you will be unable to reenter the Egyptian side. Tourists can enter from Israel at this point, and will be issued a fourteen-day pass limiting them to the east coast of the Sinai peninsula as far as Sharm el-Sheikh in the south and St. Catherine's in the west. This pass can be exchanged for a normal tourist visa at the police intelligence office in Sharm el-Sheikh.

When Israel returned the rest of Sinai to Egypt in 1982, it refused to relinquish Taba, where construction had begun on what was to become the Sonesta (now the Hilton) hotel. While both Israelis and Egyptians hunted through the archives to secure claims for ownership of the land, negotiations on its future were delayed by worsening relations between the two countries over the 1982 invasion of Lebanon. Talks were resumed early in 1985 and continued until a final package—including compensation of $38.2 million for the hotel—was agreed in February 1989. The Israelis finally withdrew from Taba on March 15, leaving the 326-room Sonesta hotel to continue temporarily under its original management until it was taken over later in the year by Hilton International.

After the settlement of the Taba dispute the border was moved back by one kilometer, so that the Hilton is now incorporated into Egyptian territory. The new Egyptian border post is one hundred yards beyond the hotel; one hundred yards beyond that is the Israeli border. Taxis, however, are still stationed at the former border post, so if you are coming from Israel and wish to avoid walking one kilometer with your luggage and diving gear you should arrange through an agent in Israel for a car to meet you at the new border.

Appendix

Useful Addresses in Cairo

Cairo Divers
Cairo Divers is open to everyone interested in diving and in the conservation of the Red Sea coast. Members enjoy discounts in certain dive clubs and hotels. Slide shows, talks, and information on diving trips, courses, and many more activities. Equipment is available for hire to members. Meetings held in the Ballroom on the second floor of the Semiramis Intercontinental Hotel on the first Monday of every month at 7:30 P.M. Diving courses at all levels can be taken in Cairo, with instruction at the swimming pool beside the el-Borg Hotel followed by a weekend in Sharm el-Sheikh or Hurghada. Contact Cairo Divers for details.

Paskalis
Kiros Paskalis runs a dive shop and center in Cairo which is convenient for anyone who might wish to take a full tank to an area of the coast with no dive center. Imported equipment for sale or hire. 6 Mohammed Helmi Ibrahim Street, off Champollion Street, Cairo. Telephone: 751908.

Dive Tour Companies Outside Egypt

Twickers World
Tours to Hurghada and Sharm el-Sheikh; guests stay in the Sheraton and Giftun Village in Hurghada; in the Ghazala, Sanafir, Marina Sharm, and Aquamarine Hotels in Sharm el-Sheikh. Dive club: Sinai Hotels and Diving Clubs, Cairo. Safaris. 22 Church Street, Twickenham, Middlesex TW1 3NW U.K. Telephone: 01-892-7606.

Oonasdivers UK
Run by Red Sea enthusiast Amanda Levick. Guests are flown to Cairo and on to Sharm el-Sheikh. Further sightseeing is encouraged. Guests stay in the Sanafir, Fayrouz Hilton, and Marina Sharm hotels. Dive club: Camel Dive Club, Na'ama Bay, with its own club in the pipe line. Cairo office: Oonas Tours, 32 Baron Street, Heliopolis. Telephone: 668747. U.K. address: 23 Enys Road, Eastbourne, Sussex BN21 2DG, U.K. Telephone: (0323) 648924.

Red Sea Aquarians
In London, representative Chris Chadwick sends tours to Hurghada through Cairo (Luxor optional). In Hurghada, Rudi and Somaya Kneip operate two 20-meter fishing boats and three dive boats purpose-built by local fishermen. Experienced divers only. Summer trips to Brothers Islands (five days) and Ras Banas (usually a nine-day, two-boat convoy). All-year-round trips include the lower western coast of the Gulf of Suez, from Shadwan Island up to Gubal. Also trips to Ras Mohammed (five days—weather permitting). Guests use the Hurghada Sheraton, Giftun Village, Abu Nawas, or club accommodation. Hill House, 94 Foxley Lane, Purley, Surrey CR2 3NA, U.K. Telephone: (01) 668 6505.

Duncan Travel
A tour operator rather than travel agent, Duncan Holloway runs a combination of sightseeing and diving holidays to Luxor and Hurghada. Beginners and experienced divers. Guests stay at the Ramoza or at Moon Valley. Dive club: Scuba-Doo, Hurghada. P.O. Box 4, Hythe, Southampton SO4 6YF, U.K. Telephone: (0703) 702063.

Jumping Goat Expeditions
A comprehensive two-week tour that includes two days at the Mena House in Cairo, five days of boat diving between Hurghada

and Sharm el-Sheikh, two days in Dahab, and a trip to St. Catherine's. Accommodation is on the boat apart from in Cairo and Dahab. Dive center: Hani Minyawi, Hurghada. Travel agent: South Sinai Travel. U.K. address: P.O. Box 295, Oxford OX2 7SF, U.K. Telephone: (0865) 516227.

Dive & Sail
Boat charter holidays. Divers board the schooner *Jarata* in Eilat and leave immediately to spend six full days diving the Sinai coast down to Ras Mohammed. At the end of the week they are dropped off at Sharm el-Sheikh and taken by bus to Taba. A trip to St. Catherine's can be included. Commons Corner, Burleigh, Nr. Stroud, Gloucester GL5 2SN, U.K. Telephone: (0453) 882267.

SUBEX
SUBEX runs diving holidays to its branch in Hurghada, where guests are accommodated in a comfortable clubhouse. Head office: Bettenstrasse 31, CH–4123 Nallschwil, Switzerland. Telephone: (061) 63 07 82/42 64 75. Telex: 965704 CH.

Long-Distance Transportation
to Red Sea Coast and Sinai

Air Travel

Air Sinai (flights to Hurghada, St. Catherine's, Sharm el-Sheikh, and el-Tor): office at Nile Hilton, telephone: 760948; and other Cairo locations.

EgyptAir (flights to Hurghada): office at Nile Hilton, telephone: 759806/703; and throughout city and in all major tourist destinations.

Zas Passenger Service (flights to Hurghada and St. Catherine's): office at Novotel, Cairo International Airport Road, telephone: 291-8032.

Also note that weekly charter flights arrive in Hurghada from Stuttgart and Munich, and during the winter season five charter flights a week arrive in Sharm el-Sheikh from Germany, Austria, and Switzerland.

Bus Travel

It is not normally necessary to reserve in advance, but allow plenty of time when buying a ticket (in Cairo, at least two hours). Be sure to check that your ticket is for the correct departure time and day, as no refunds can be made. Also note that women are often waved to the front of the queue.

To Hurghada Tickets can be obtained at Travco Shark el-Delta offices at Midan Ahmed Helmi, north of Ramses Station in Cairo. Buses leave daily (except Friday) from the station in Abbassia.

Upper Egyptian Bus Company buses leave from the terminal in Midan Ahmed Helmi (offices at 4 Yusuf Abbas, Madinat Nasr, telephone: 260-9304/9297/9298, at terminal: 746658)

To Sinai Tickets to Dahab, Nuweiba, St. Catherine's, Sharm el-Sheikh, and Dahab can be bought at the East Delta Bus Company offices at 4 Tayaran, Madinat Nasr, Cairo (telephone: 261-1882/3/5/6). Buses leave from the Sinai bus terminal in Abbassia.

To Suez Tickets can be bought at East Delta Bus Company offices. Buses leave regularly from the East Delta Bus Company terminal at el-Kulali (by the underpass to Shubra).

Ferries

From Hurghada to Sharm el-Sheikh An occasional service. The trip each way takes 6 hours. Inquire in Hurghada through any of the hotels, at Les Voyages (opposite the Red Sea restaurant, open daily from 9:00 A.M. to 1:00 P.M. and from 4:00 P.M. to 9:00 P.M., telephone: (062) 440184; telex: 92750), or at Sea Cruisers Travel (Main Street, open daily 8:00 A.M. to 2:00 P.M. and 5:00 P.M. to 9:00 P.M., telephone: 440282).

From Nuweiba to Aqaba The first ferry leaves daily at 11:00 A.M., arriving in Aqaba at 2:00 P.M.; the second leaves Nuweiba at 6 p.m. From Aqaba the ferries leave at 11:00 A.M. and 4:00 P.M. (expect long delays). Egyptians and foreigners resident in Egypt for more than five years should expect to pay slightly more for a first-class ticket than tourists, because tourist tickets are not subject to taxation. The cost of transporting cars is in accordance with their size. Bookings may be made in Cairo at the

Egyptian Navigation Company, 26 Sherif St. (right on the corner of Sherif and Kasr el-Nil). Telephone: 745598.

From Sharm el-Sheikh to Hurghada Inquire at South Sinai Travel, Ghazala Hotel, Na'ama Bay.

From Suez to Aqaba and beyond A ferry leaves at noon for Aqaba on Wednesdays and Saturdays. The journey takes 17 hours; there are first- and second-class cabins (the latter with shared bathrooms). Egyptians and foreigners with residency of more than five years must pay a tax surcharge in Egyptian pounds which could amount to one-third of the price of the ticket. From Aqaba buses leave for Amman, Baghdad, Damascus, Kuwait, and Saudi Arabia. Ferry tickets can be obtained in advance from Mena Tours, 14 Talaat Harb Street, Cairo. Telephone: 740864/740955/776951.

Four-Wheel Drive

Four-wheel drive jeeps can be hired from Max Rent-a-Car, 27 Lebanon Street, Mohandiseen, Cairo. Telephone: 3474712/ 3474713.

Service Taxis

From Cairo to Suez: leaving from behind Ramses railway station at a fare of LE 2.

Historical Sources
and Further Reading

Historical Sources

Baedeker, Karl. *Lower Egypt (and the Peninsula of Sinai)*. Leipzig: K. Baedeker, 1878.

———. *Egypt* 4th ed. Leipzig: K. Baedeker, 1898.

Daumas, J. *La Péninsule du Sinaï*. Cairo: Royal Automobile Club d'Egypte, 1951.

Flaubert, Gustave. *Flaubert in Egypt: A Sensibility on Tour*. Translated and edited by Francis Steegmuller. Chicago: Academy Chicago Ltd., 1979.

Forbin, Louis Nicolas Philippe Auguste, Comte de. *Travels in Egypt: Being a Continuation of the Travels in the Holy Land in 1817–1818 by Comte de Forbin*. London: Sir Richard Philippe, 1819

Jarvis, C. S. *Desert and Delta*. London: John Murray, 1938.

———. *Three Deserts*. London: John Murray, 1936.

Kammerer, M. Albert. *La Mer Rouge, l'Abyssinie et l'Arabie depuis l'antiquité.* Cairo: Société Royale de géographie d'Égypte, 1929.

Monfreid, Henri de. *Hashish: Smuggling under Sail in the Red Sea.* London: Methuen & Co., 1935.

Montulé, Edward de. *Travels in Egypt in 1818 & 1819.* London: Geographical Society, 1819.

United Kingdom, Naval Intelligence Division. *Western Arabia and the Red Sea.* Geographical Handbook Series. Oxford: University Press under the authority of H.M. Stationery Office, 1946.

Further Reading

Cohen, Shlomo. *Red Sea Diver's Guide.* Tel Aviv: Seapen Books, 1988. [An excellent guidebook not available in Egypt.]

Deuvletian, Roupen. *Red Sea Fish Guide.* Cairo: Nubar Printing House, 1988.

Hazleton, Lesley. *Where Mountains Roar.* New York: Holt, Rinehart and Winston, 1980.

Megalli, Mary Dungan. *On the Road in Egypt: A Motorist's Guide.* Cairo: The American University in Cairo Press, 1989.

Randall, John E. *Diver's Guide to Red Sea Fishes.* Waterproof ed. London: Immel Publishing Ltd., 1986.

———. *Red Sea Reef Fishes.* London: Immel Publishing Ltd., 1986.

———. *Sharks of Arabia.* London: Immel Publishing Ltd., 1986.

Vine, Peter. *Red Sea Invertebrates.* London: Immel Publishing Ltd., 1986.

———. *Red Sea Safety: A Guide to Dangerous Marine Animals.* London: Immel Publishing Ltd., 1986.

Vine, Peter, and Hagen Schmid. *Red Sea Explorers.* London: Immel Publishing Ltd., 1987.

Index